CONFES of a GIG-GOER

Celebrating 50 Years of Live Concerts

To Mum,

with much love

David

David Parker

Published by New Generation Publishing in 2024

Copyright © David Parker 2024

First Edition

The author asserts the moral right under the Copyright, Designs and Patents Act 1988 to be identified as the author of this work.

All Rights reserved. No part of this publication may be reproduced, stored in a retrieval system or transmitted, in any form or by any means without the prior consent of the author, nor be otherwise circulated in any form of binding or cover other than that which it is published and without a similar condition being imposed on the subsequent purchaser.

Paperback ISBN: 9781835631997

www.newgeneration-publishing.com

Contents

Page

Introduction

- Opening Confessions — 5
- Gig-going Musings — 7
- Community Connections — 10
- Glamorous Beginnings — 12

The 1970s - Chapters 1 – 9 — 15

The 1980s - Chapters 10 – 38 — 56

The 1990s - Chapters 39 – 42 — 155

The 2000s - Chapters 43 – 52 — 180

The 2010s - Chapters 53 – 74 — 206

The 2020s - Chapters 75 – 80 — 267

Epilogue – Closing Confessions — 293

Appendices — 296

- My Top 3s
- Index of Bands seen live
- Acknowledgements

Confession Digressions

	Page
Ticket Confessions	27
Tout Confessions	114
Live Aid Confessions	131
Set list Confessions	140
Glitter Confessions	168
Faith Confessions	189
Wave Confessions	218
Health Confessions	246
Covid Confessions	275

Introduction

Opening Confessions

My first confession is that despite producing a book on the subject, I don't profess to be an afficionado in rock/popular music. I have pockets of interest in which I have reasonable knowledge, but my overall 'across the board' comprehension is not great to say the least. Nor do I profess to be in any sense the 'ultimate' gig-goer. Compared to some people, my concert tally bears no comparison. In fact, one of my gig-going companions goes to see as many bands in a month as I do in a year.

But I can confess that over the years my love for music and especially the live gig has continued to grow. The year 2023 marked fifty years since my musical journey began, and 2025 clocks half a century of 'gig-going'.

Over this time span, I will readily confess to having been fortunate to see many of the top artists and bands the world has produced. The myriad of memories that they have created, I have attempted to document in this book.

I hope you enjoy re-living them with me.

Finally, I confess that whilst I have been to the odd gig on my own, almost all have been alongside others – my family, friends, school & uni mates, work colleagues etc. Many I have lost touch with, yet for each unique gig, the person(s) I have queued with, stood alongside, or sat next to, I have shared, in that moment, at that time, the one-off experience that each live gig brings.

So, I dedicate this book to all of you gig-goers, wherever you may be, who at one time or another have clapped, chanted and sung your heart out beside me and with me.

I thank you all...

Gig-Going Musings

Ponder on these thoughts for a while.

From the moment you buy a ticket to a gig, you are immediately yet intangibly connected to a group of people you have never met. People from different cities, countries, nationalities, cultures, ages, backgrounds & personalities. The high majority you would perhaps never meet in 'your circle' nor would you necessarily actively seek to meet – but the connection exists by each person having bought a ticket for the same show at the same venue on the same night as you.

From here on in, you embark on a similar pathway. This starts with what I have come to recognise as 'The Journey of Anticipation', a process that a gig-goer experiences between ticket purchase and event. Now obviously this 'journey' varies from person to person. For the casual attendee or inquisitive onlooker, this can be minimal. Perhaps it consists of a simple entry in the diary and then it's forgotten until the week of the event.

However, for fans and followers of a performer, the process of anticipation can be intense; something that can be quite delicious yet agonising at the same time. Agonising because sometimes the length of time between ticket purchase and event is often six months to a year, sometimes longer. That is a lot of waiting. But it can also be delicious because the nearer you get, the more the excitement builds.

I have in my younger days embarked on the countdown by physically ticking off the calendar and/or mentally counting down the days. Anticipation also has been built by delving more into the band you now have an appointment with. This occurs by maybe re-acquainting yourself with songs that you haven't heard in a while, getting to know a new album or investigating an unfamiliar back catalogue.

But here's the strange thing. In this very process, you have become part of something communal – joining with hundreds and sometimes thousands of others – waiting.

And then when the day eventually arrives, something extraordinary begins to happen...

As an example – picture this scenario:

Imagine you bought a ticket for a big concert to see one of your favourite bands at Wembley Stadium. Now picture in your mind a large map of the UK and on that map, you can see Wembley in North West London, represented with a large coloured light. Now imagine that everyone who has also bought a ticket (including you), appears on the map as a small individual white light located in their homes wherever they live.

What would the map look like?

Well quite simply there would probably be white lights everywhere – up to 90,000 maybe.[1] The largest group of lights would likely be in and around London and then spreading out all over the country, obviously becoming less in number the further away you get from the venue. But you can bet there would be some lights down in Cornwall, some up in Scotland and if you went into Europe some lights would be there and even further afield still.

---

[1] **The Capacity of Wembley Stadium**

As you make your way to the venue on the long-awaited day, your light on the map starts to move from where you live towards the large coloured light of Wembley. At this point it probably never crosses your mind that there are 89,999 other lights mobilising and heading towards the same destination.

Then as you get closer, you start to recognise others on that same journey. At tube stops people join your train with t-shirts bearing the band's name. You can glean excitement on their faces and perhaps for the first time you are reminded you are part of something much bigger. And then as you exit the train at Wembley Tube Station, you're aware you have arrived as you join a throng of fellow gig-goers all now closing in on their destination. There is a tangible sense of eager expectation which continues to grow as you move onward with the crowd, passing food vendors and t-shirt sellers. As the venue comes into view and you undertake the 'Wembley walk' up to the stadium entrances, you become like numerous streams merging into a river of people (or maybe we could say a sea of lights) flowing towards an inevitable indescribable something that is to happen right here, this very day. As you enter the packed stadium and take your place you drink in the sights, sounds and sensations going on all around you. Once more the picture of the map enters your mind... now the large light of Wembley and the 90,000 small lights... have almost naturally, become one.

And then finally the show is ready to begin...

Community Connections.

One of the things I love most about gig-going is this sense of gathering as a community — this feeling of oneness, togetherness. You may go to a gig alone, but when you're there, there's a sense that you are never alone.

As human beings we have an intrinsic need to belong. We need a community. We need communion and connection with others.

The online world we live in, despite many benefits, has created a world where many people socialise in isolation, which can easily create a counterfeit sense of community, and lead to loneliness and depression[2], the very opposite result than intended.

It's foolish to even suggest a music concert fulfils the human need to any lasting degree. But it does in some ways, point the way. The joy of a great gig is the experience of this sense of unity, of connection to the band, the music, the songs and to each other. When 90,000 people belt out an iconic song in unison, there is a power that can transport the soul to new heights.

---

[2] A study published in JAMA Psychiatry showed that adolescents who spend more than three hours daily on social media had heightened risks of psychological and mental health issues, including loneliness, depression, and suicide.

"On a really great night, you are the crowd and the crowd is you. That can really happen... The audience, and Edge, Adam, Larry & I have disappeared into each other. There is no them, only us".

Bono [3]

---

[3] **Quote from ''Surrender', the life story of U2's Bono published by Hutchinson Heinemann 2022. A recommended read.**

Glamorous Beginnings.

So where did this all begin for me?

I was a '70s kid' as far as music goes.

Born in 1960, my memories of the music scene or indeed any historical or cultural events from this decade are very vague.

My parents loved the theatre (especially musicals) and variety shows, but had little interest in popular music. So, in my first decade of life, I have no recollection of seeing or hearing bands like the Beatles or the Stones, either on records, radio or the black and white TV we had.

The first record I owned, which was bought for me in the late 1960s (by my grandparents I think), was *'Lily the Pink'* by The Scaffold, an excellent novelty sing-along song, which was obviously the appeal.

Rock n' roll is generally thought to have been born in the USA in the early to mid-1950s, but my own birth into rock music occurred in 1973, the year I entered into my teens.

For Christmas 1972, I had been given a Vinyl LP *'20 Fantastic Hits by the Original Artists – Volume 2'* [4] the second of three compilation albums by Arcade

---

[4] I still have this LP, and looking at the track list now there were some great tracks included: 'Hot Love' by T-Rex, 'Delta Lady' by Joe Cocker and 'Layla' by Derek and the Dominoes (Eric Clapton's band at the time).

Records[5]. My favourite track on this LP was *'Little Willy'* by *The Sweet*, which I recall playing over and over again.

Of course, if you wanted to keep up with the music scene, essential viewing was the weekly TV programme *'Top of the Pops'*. This was broadcast every Thursday evening and included a countdown of the Top 30 selling singles of the week. I started watching TOTP avidly around the start of 1973 and in one of the first episodes I saw, performing a new single called *'Blockbuster'* was none other than The Sweet.

This song was different from anything I'd ever heard before – impacting both musically and visually, and obviously I was not alone as the following week the single went straight to No 1 and stayed there for several weeks.

A musical movement was underway, termed 'glam rock'. It had several pioneers with artists like Slade, Wizzard, Gary Glitter and T.Rex among the forerunners. Other legendary artists that perhaps wouldn't normally be labelled in the 'glam' category, nevertheless had roots in this movement, were David Bowie, Alice Cooper, Queen and Elton John.

---

[5] **Arcade Records was founded in 1972 by Laurence Myers in response to Music listeners starting to create mix-tapes of current top hits. '20 Fantastic Hits' was the first and most popular of many similar releases, most of which were destined to end up in 50p bins in Charity Shops in the 2020s.**

Brian Connolly
a Lesson in layered hair

But if you had to choose one band that were the epitome of the glam rock revolution, it would have to be The Sweet. Make-up, sequins, eyeliner, outrageous costumes, platform shoes, lipstick, voluptuous hairstyles and glitter a-plenty – they had it all.

As a thirteen-year-old I remember wanting a hairstyle like lead singer Brian Connolly – blonde shoulder length hair that curled in around the face. *"It's layered"*, my Mum explained, *"that's why it curls in."*

So next time I went to the barbers, I asked for him to layer my hair. I'm not sure what happened, but one thing was for sure, it never looked remotely like Brian Connolly!

Of course, the glam rock craze could be partially blamed for the horrendous fashion of the 1970s. The fact that as a teenager, I went out in public wearing bell bottomed trousers with high waste bands, bright flowery shirts with matching ties, and platform shoes[6], causes me to shudder in disbelief. How such garments were allowed to exist is hard to fathom and the thought that they may come back into fashion one day brings a shiver to the spine.

Yet this was the rock n' roll scene I was born into; this is where it all began, and the rest, so they say, is history.

---

[6] I recall a pair of leather shoes I wore with a 3-tone colour – brown, maroon and orange, which were round fronted with 1" thick soles and 2" Heels!!

PART ONE
THE 1970s

Chapter 1. Omitting a Legend
Cliff Richard
Finkin St. Methodist Church, Grantham. 1974

It's even a surprise to me that this is my first gig listed. This was a late entry not initially included simply because I'd never associated the event with my gig life. But it happened and I suppose to omit seeing a legend live after actually seeing a legend live, would be a travesty.

This was a gospel tour, which Cliff regularly undertook alongside his mainstream tours to share his Christian Faith. On this particular occasion, he visited my home town Grantham in Lincolnshire, performing at two church venues there.

I remember the concerts were free, but I also recall tickets were like gold dust. I presume I managed to get one through my grandparents who were regular attenders at the Methodist church.

My memory of the event was being seated in a packed balcony, and Cliff being whisked on, performing a few songs (of which I knew none) and whisked off again straight to the second show elsewhere.

I remember hoping he would sing *'Power to all our Friends'* which he had performed the previous year in the Eurovision Song Contest (and came third) ...but no such luck.

At that time, he kept the gospel content separate from his mainstream career and the two didn't cross

(although I have heard he now has a gospel section in his arena shows.)

The event as a concert had little impact on me. It all seemed very manufactured.

What it needed was a bit of glam...

So, let's move onto Chapter 2.

Chapter 2. Screaming Girls
The Glitter Band.
The Palace, Newark 1975.

The Glitter Band hit the glam rock scene in 1973. They were originally the backing band for Gary Glitter, but emerged as an independent separate act due to a string of catchy singles.

The gig was advertised in our local paper, (Newark being a half hour's drive away from Grantham.) From the first sighting of the advert, I begged my parents to get tickets, and almost to my surprise – they did! My excitement was tangible. My Dad tried to wind me up with comments like *"I don't know why you want to go - it'll be full of screaming girls."*

"Don't be silly Dad," I remember dismissively responding, *"it's not the Bay City Rollers."*[7] But I confess I really had no idea what to expect.

So, on the 21st April 1975, age 14, I had my first experience of a rock gig (with my parents).

I recall our seats were about half way back. The audience had some diversity but the high majority were teenage girls, faces covered in glitter and wardrobes to match. Dad at one point leant forward, looked toward me, nodded towards a couple of the 'glam girls' and winked. I knew what he meant and I shook my head to reinforce that this was no 'Rollers' show!

---

[7] **Scottish Boy Band who breathed fresh life into Tartan. They were Teen Pop Idols and 'Rollermania' worldwide probably equaled Beatlemania in levels of hysteria, which meant yes...they had screaming girls wherever they went.**

The support band were called 'Fogg', standard hard rock and loud. If it was loud for me, goodness knows how my folks were finding it. When I looked towards them, I'm sure I discerned notable grimacing.

Then after a break, it was time. The lights went out, dry ice covered the stage, the unmistakable 'glitter' drum sound pounded forth, and there appeared the band launching into the opening song.

Immediately, there was mass movement. All the girls leapt out of their seats and ran to the front of the stage...screaming!!

The three of us were left forming a kind of island amongst the surrounding empty seats. It felt like we had been abandoned!

There was a slight feeling of bemusement and a for a moment a 'what do we do now?' I honestly can't remember what we did do!

But the gig was fantastic. The costumes, performance, interaction, song content, singalong encore: in fact, all the ingredients of a great rock concert were there. I had experienced for the first time the power of a live show and it made its mark.

My parents were both deaf for over a week, whereas I just experienced, what was to become a familiar companion in any gig aftermath – the ringing in the ears.

Of course, I had to eat humble pie over the screaming. *"Didn't I say..."* began Dad as soon as we got in the car after the show. *"Yes, you did..."* I cut him off immediately ...and no more was said.

I knew Dad had hated the show yet as I glanced at his face in the driving mirror from the back seat on the way home, I couldn't help but perceive a slightly smug, self-satisfied grin of contentment.

Chapter 3. A True Royal Occasion
Queen
Earls Court London. 1977

November 20th 1975 was a significant day. It was on this day that I was introduced to the band that has most influenced my musical journey over the years.

This particular day was the day that *'Bohemian Rhapsody'* first appeared on *'Top of the Pops'*. I remember it so well, simply because I had never seen or heard anything like it before.

Bear in mind the groundbreaking fact that this was the first time a video[8] had been directly used to promote a song.

I confess I didn't know what to make of this visual and musical extravaganza...and I was not alone.

The next day at school there was only one topic of conversation with one leading question: *Did you see Top of the Pops?*

Discussion was rife. Some loved it, some hated it but most were simply in the valley of indecision.

One week later the verdict had been reached. Possibly helped by Capital Radio DJ Kenny Everett playing the song fourteen times in two days, *Bohemian Rhapsody* soared straight to No 1, and remained there for nine weeks over Christmas 1975 and into the New year of '76. The accompanying LP *'A Night at the*

---

[8] Apparently, this took only a few hours to film and cost £4,500. It was shown on TOTP only 10 days after filming completed

Opera' also topped the album charts and to cap it all, the band's final show of their UK tour, at the Hammersmith Odeon was broadcast live on TV as a Christmas Eve special.

In early 1976, one of my best mates told me he had decided to buy *'A Night at the Opera'*. I had had a similar idea with record tokens[9] I'd been given for Christmas. So, we both headed into town one Saturday morning. We came up with the genius idea that as opposed to us both buying the same record, why not buy different ones and share the contents? So, my friend bought *'A Night at the Opera'* and I bought *'Queen 2'* despite not knowing any songs.

To this day *'Queen 2'*, along with their last album *'Made in Heaven'*, remain my favourites.

My appreciation for the band continued to grow and by mid 1976, I was familiar with all four Queen albums released to date, and eager for the next, which appeared at the end of the year - *'A Day at the Races'*, the title like its predecessor taken from a Marx Brothers movie.

However, excitement spiraled with an announcement of some shows in 1977. I first found out through one of the popular weekly music mags (Record Mirror, Sounds, Melody Maker) – I can't remember which one, but the whole back page was

---

[9] Ahhh… those were the days. Record tokens! The safe bet gift that always sufficed when you didn't know what else to buy or you'd left things to the last minute.

devoted to two shows at Earl's Court in June (the first was already sold out and a second date had been added.) However, I needed to persuade my parents somehow to give me permission to go, which initially didn't look great. The date advertised with ticket availability was a Tuesday night which meant a school day plus the problem of transport to London.

But then came a crucial discovery.

I realised that these dates had been deliberately planned by the band to coincide with Queen Elizabeth's Silver Jubilee, and June 7th was the actual day of celebration.[10]

A public holiday was announced on the Tuesday along with celebration details which included a royal carriage procession through London. It was this royal occasion that enabled me to swing a day in London on June 7th with my parents to see the Jubilee celebration parade during the day and for me and a mate to go to the gig at night.

The next obstacle was getting the tickets.

Younger readers need to be reminded that at this time there were no online ticket sites, or indeed online anything. Nor was there box office or ticket phone lines to ring and reserve seats with a credit card. No Sir! It was writing a cheque (or if you were really unlucky and had no access to a cheque book, getting a postal order from the nearest post office) for the correct amount and sending it off with a stamped addressed envelope

---

[10] I later found out the proceeds for this show went to the Queen's Silver Jubilee Appeal – a nice touch!

so the tickets could be sent to you. Or if sold out, your cheque/ PO sent back to you.

Off went my cheque for the dizzy sum of £9 (that was two tickets at £4 plus 50p admin fee each), and after about four weeks wait, my own handwritten envelope arrived through the letterbox. My nerves turned to ecstatic celebration as I opened the envelope and out fell two Queen tickets.

EARLS COURT, LONDON
(Opposite Warwick Road Exit, Earls Court Tube Station)

Harvey Goldsmith and John Reid
cordially invite you to a night with

Queen

BLOCK
9

TUESDAY, 7th JUNE, 1977
at 8.00 p.m.

Ground Floor Stalls £4.00

D79

For Conditions of Sale see over — To be retained

The coming months introduced me for the first time to this almost unique feeling (one that became familiar over the years) of anticipation and excitement, growing day by day as the time marched (far too slowly) towards gig date. But eventually the day arrived... June 7th 1977.

Despite the amazing spectacle and wonderful atmosphere of the royal procession, nothing compared to what I experienced at Earl's Court, which was, my first arena gig.

As I reflect back on the many concerts I have attended over the years, this show still resonates as one of the best gigs ever. It was such an awe-inspiring show. I think my senses were on overload trying to take in the visual feast whilst engaging in the music. Certain things are firmly lodged in my memory in a much bolder sense than more recent gigs. Unforgettable moments were:

1. The Start.

As the lights went out, the instrumental opener from Queen 2, *'Procession',* blasted from the speakers.[11] Then a massive lighting rig in the shape of a crown covering the stage, slowly started to rise,[12] ascending majestically amidst a deep rumbling with the dry ice pouring forth. It was like a launching rocket. Suddenly, with an explosion of light, the band appeared out of the smoke on the stage with the opening riffs of the new album's first track, *'Tie your Mother Down.'* Astonishing! [c/f Appendix A:7]

2. Freddie's numerous costumes

I think it was five or six changes from the judo suit to the silver lurex glitter sequined one-piece leotard (which also appeared on future tours) and of course, the famous Harlequin leotard which was inspired by the legendary ballet

The Harlequin suit... a dainty little number

---

[11] This was a special intro as a nod towards the silver jubilee procession. Apparently, it was never used again.

[12] This was a pioneering piece of apparatus for the time - the mobile lighting unit. I'm not sure if this was the first time such a contraption was ever used but certainly it broke new ground. It was over fifty foot tall, weighed two tonnes and cost the band £50,000 for the two Earl's Court shows.

dancer Nijinsky.[13] I recall a review of the concert in a music mag the following week with the headline, *'Was this a Concert or a fashion show?'*

3. Being moved to tears during *'White Queen'*
As this gentle song built towards its powerful climax and Freddie's voice soared to new heights with such power, my soul was touched and moved.

4. A version of *Jailhouse Rock* as a final encore
with Freddie in another outrageous outfit.

This was my first live 'Queen' experience, and an unforgettable, mind-blowing piece of musical theatre, full of pomp and ceremony; a worthy tribute to the day's royal celebrations. Over the coming years, I was fortunate to see 'Queen' with Freddie eight times. (See Chapters 9 & 33). With the exception of Wembley Stadium in 1986, this night at Earl's Court was unsurpassed.

---

[13] **This outfit sold for £22,500 at an auction in 2012. A bargain considering Freddie's arrow jacket worn at the Milton Keynes bowl went for £203,200 in the high-profile Sotheby's auction in 2023**

Ticket Confessions

I confess that I'm a bit of a ticket geek.

Once upon a time I bought a piece of paper. I paid £4 for it. This can seem a lot for a piece of paper measuring 11.5cm x 7.5cm.

But that piece of paper enabled me to occupy seat D79 in Block 9 in Earls Court on a Tuesday evening in June in 1977. From when it arrived in the post to the date of the show, that piece of paper was way more valuable to me than £4 – it seemed priceless!

But after the show is over, the ticket stub that was needed to gain entrance expires. It is no longer valid. So, most people without second thought simply threw them away. After all, they're worth nothing after the event. Right?

Not exactly! Gig tickets have become collectable items in the world of rock n' roll memorabilia. They represent to punters a relatively affordable item to collect, whether it be a favourite band, a legendary show or a gig that was personally attended.

Think about it – venues have a capacity, so tickets to any event have a finite supply. For venues with reserved seating each ticket represents a different seat, so each ticket is in fact unique, representing a small piece of popular music history.

On a more personal note, a simple ticket stub can act like a portal back in time to re-ignite precious memories of times past.

The stub becomes proof of a memory: 'I was there.'

Every ticket tells a story!

I confess that I have always tended to hold on to most of my ticket stubs and in true geeky fashion, I stuck them in a book alongside the set list which I wrote out from memory after each gig.

Sellotape, I later discovered, is not a ticket's best friend, and caused permanent brown stains. So, I carefully and gradually moved them to a proper ticket album, which in equally geeky fashion has a transparent plastic slot to display and protect the ticket and a few lines alongside to write notes, thoughts and memories of the event. In fact, a sort of condensed version of this book.

Sadly today, the online world we live in means hard copy tickets in themselves are becoming less common. Today if you buy online, it usually results in 'electronic' tickets being sent direct to your inbox or mobile, with a barcode that is shown and scanned on entry. Very easy but potentially damaging to geeks who have albums for tickets!

As with all things that tend to become victims of technology, I'm sure they will be back, just like vinyl and cassette tapes have re-appeared once again after disappearing for a few years.

By the way, I scoured E bay and an original Earl's Court ticket stub that cost me £4 in 1977, was selling for over £100.

Who would have thought it?

Chapter 4. Punk Pandemonium
The Jam
Kings Hall Derby 1977

The punk movement was gaining rapid momentum at this time. Its foundation birthed out of anger and disgruntlement from an emerging generation of teens and youth, faced with issues of unemployment, inflation, strikes and the seeming increasing divide between rich and poor. Punk rock suddenly presented a platform enabling young people to have a voice, to be heard, to protest against political and social norms and most significantly, an 'arena' to vent their frustrations.

This gave rise to a whole stream of new bands rising up to produce the aggressive, raw, abrasive, angry sound that characterised this genre. The interesting reality about producing punk music was that you didn't have to be any good. In fact, sometimes the worse a band was musically, the better. That's because a gig primarily was not to admire the artist, it was to let loose, to vent those pent-up frustrations with no holds barred. All that was needed was a loud distorted noise, and many bands were happy to oblige.

However as with everything the cream rises to the top, and there were bands that were good at being bad. The Sex Pistols led the way, managed brilliantly by Malcolm McClaren, whose tactics seemed to be to rebel against anything that was the norm, and do whatever necessary to create outrage. This was brought about by an offensive album cover, songs about destroying the social order, bad language at inappropriate times, and even using stolen equipment for their gigs. The Sex Pistols stood as non-conformist revolutionaries, which in many ways was what defined the punk movement. It wasn't long before they were banned from the airwaves, the charts and most venues. '*<u>And we don't care...</u>*' they screamed on their single *'Pretty Vacant'* – and they didn't, because it all led to more 'success'.

But there were punk bands that did care. The Clash and The Ramones spring to mind, and The Jam were another. Led by guitarist/vocalist Paul Weller with Bruce Foxton on bass and Rick Butler on drums, this three piece band were a little different in style. For one thing, The Jam didn't dress 'punk' – instead they were arrayed in tight matching suits and narrow ties, which never seemed to hinder their popularity.

Personally, I never gave much value to the punk rock movement at that time. However, when a couple of friends from my school sixth form organised a bus trip to Derby for this gig and there was space, I signed up.

The first thing I noticed on entry was that about half the crowd were punks with their trademark appearance – coloured mohawks, ripped clothing, DMs, piercings, accessories with spikes and safety pins everywhere. The dress, of course, was just one example of the rebellious nature of punk, which worked in the exact opposite way to society. So, what was deemed culturally as anti-social behaviour, tended to become the accepted norm for punk rockers. For example, throwing things and spitting (or gobbing as it was known) at the bands playing, were seen by punks as acts of approval.

As soon as support band New Hearts went on stage, the pandemonium began. The punks charged to the front and started 'pogoing' (jumping up and down) in an uncontrolled manner. About six songs in, the lead vocalist got 'bottled,' and with blood running down his head, the whole band retreated off stage, to loud approving cheers.

To say security was sparse is somewhat of an understatement. Thinking back, I remember seeing some personnel protecting the stage, but I don't recall any audience intervention.

When The Jam came on stage, the moshing/pogoing went wild at the front. I mean arms were flailing, fists were randomly flying, people were getting hit and going down but nobody seemed to care. Getting hurt seemed to be part of the deal. People were climbing up the stage barrier or sides and leaping full on back into the crowd. It made the crowd surfing that I sometimes see at gigs today seem like a teddy bear's picnic!

But the worst had to be the already mentioned revolting habit of spitting/gobbing on the band. However, this now traditional response of a sign of favour was not appreciated by those being spat on. Weller in between songs: *'Will you stop doing that, we don't f**^*g like it'*.

It didn't seem to make much difference.

They played a high velocity forty-five minute set with tracks from debut album '*In the City*' and new follow up LP *'Modern World'*. The energy the band gave off on stage was phenomenal.

We stayed well on the periphery safe out of harm's way and actually had a great time.

The Jam became one of the few punk bands to accomplish the transition to main stream chart success. They enjoyed huge popularity having eighteen consecutive top 40 hits and four No 1's including *'Going Underground'* and *'A Town called Malice'*. Their songs became a bit more *'pop'* but they never abandoned their core aggressive sound.

They split up at the end of 1982 somewhat unharmoniously. Paul Weller went on to form *'The Style Council'* the following year and then in 1989, launched a solo career. Now almost fifty years on from the days of 'The Jam', he has achieved almost legendary status as a musical and social icon. He is today affectionately known as *'The Modfather'*.

Bruce Foxton heads a band called 'From the Jam' and keeps the songs alive.

For me, I confess this gig was the only genuine full on punk gig I've ever been to and for that reason, one that very much sticks in the memory.

ENDALE CONCERTS
present

KING'S HALL — DERBY

FRIDAY, 25th NOVEMBER, 1977

JAM

SUPPORT

Tickets £1.70

Nº 00044

Chapter 5. Rock Bottom
UFO
*Nottingham Playhouse 1978 &
De Montford Hall, Leicester 1979*

UFO are one of the great British rock bands having now surpassed 50 years on the scene. They have produced 22 albums and whilst never hitting the heights of headlining large arenas, they have been a backbone band through the decades, mainly thanks to vocalist Phil Mogg, who despite constant line-up changes, remained the lynchpin throughout.

Everyone into rock music at my school loved this band. Not only was there a flamboyant and skilful bass player in the form of Pete Way, but a quite brilliant lead guitarist called Michael Schenker, his 'Flying V' guitar and his solos, often the talking point around the band. The classic track *'Rock Bottom'* presented a showcase for him and a platform for serious air guitar exploits for us.

My first live experience of UFO was through another organised school event seeing them at the Nottingham Playhouse. At this point I knew very little of their stuff, but went on recommendation to see Schenker play live.

What I most remember about this gig was how inappropriate the venue was for the band. To be fair, there was little choice in Nottingham for rock venues in the 70s, but the Playhouse was specifically designed for theatre and plays: fixed seating, flat in the stalls and steeply tiered in the balcony. Great for enjoying a production sitting down. Trouble was who wants to sit down at a UFO gig?

As soon as the band took to the stage, half the crowd in the stalls stood up but were immediately instructed to sit down again by ushers in bow ties. Observing from a balcony seat, the next 30 minutes involved an off-stage battle between a frustrated audience and the venue's bow-tied stewards, with the latter racing from one pocket to another to keep the crowd seated. This then became a game with one group of people waiting until the stewards were as far away from their section before standing! The poor staff were fighting a losing battle and the final nail in the coffin for them was when vocalist Mogg, with a deliberate innocence, announced a well-known song with *"Come on – everyone up on your feet for this one"*. Suddenly everyone was up and the officials visibly crumpled in surrender to rapturous applause from the crowd.

This was all observed from the balcony. However, standing upstairs presented another challenge. The circle seating was so steep, your feet were level with the head of the person in the row in front, which in turn meant the gap for your feet between rows was only about one foot. If you stood up and the person in front was seated, it was like standing on a precipice with an awareness of impending vertigo. Even if you overcame that, there was no room to move.

In the end, we exited the circle, and snuck into the stalls unchallenged. By this time rows of people were at the front of the stage, and we joined them for the end of the show in time to witness Schenker's *Rock Bottom* solo in all its glory.

In complete contrast was the band's sold out gig the following year in 1979 at the De Montfort Hall in Leicester. We had tickets for the stalls which was all standing. The support band were called 'Liar' who were fantastic. They had just released their second album and single entitled *'Set the World on Fire'*, and although we didn't know any of the songs, they really took off and we rocked hard.[14] So much so I was completely knackered when UFO took to the stage. I lasted about halfway through their set and had to take a breather to the side. Guitarist Paul Chapman had taken Schenker's place for this tour, and whilst an adequate replacement, fell well short when it came to the iconic solos.

Bass Player Pete Way – more energy than me

---

[14] **Liar disbanded straight after this tour**.

Chapter 6. Crossroads Moments
The Next Band & Def Leppard
Grantham Guildhall 1978

In Grantham, the town I grew up in, one of the highlights were the school discos.[15] I attended an all-boys grammar school in the town and of course there was an equivalent all girls high school. On occasions discos were arranged in non-school venues by a school or college. Sometimes live bands played, but the main purpose of these events was seen as rare and good opportunities to check out, meet and chat up the opposite sex. However, there was one occasion when the disco and 'girl pursuit' played second fiddle.

In the late '70s, a trio of sixth form boys from my school formed a rock group calling themselves 'The Next Band.' They were head and shoulders above other local bands at that time and after playing a few local gigs, they started to attract a following. They were booked to play at the 1978 end of term Christmas Disco, which was held at the Grantham Guildhall. Anticipation was high as the band were to promote a newly launched four track vinyl EP (called *'Four by Three'* - pictured over) - songs we were already familiar with. The gig lived up to expectations. The Next Band took to the small stage

---

[15] The fact that they were, probably goes some way towards explaining why Grantham was voted 'the most boring town in England' in the early 1980s

to rapturous applause, played a blinder and brought the house down in front of a large home crowd. We left that night convinced this band had a potentially bright future and next year could be the year they hit the big time.

I should mention at this stage that a reasonably late addition to proceedings that evening was the inclusion of a support band from Sheffield, a five-piece outfit called Def Leppard — which at the time I remember thinking was a bit of a naff name and much too like Led Zeppelin.

I can remember very little about them or their set except they did a couple of Thin Lizzy covers and played a song called *'Getcha Rocks off'* which I recall thinking was quite AC/DC in style.

Their appearance in Grantham came about because Next Band drummer Frank Noon [pictured left on record sleeve] had played on the newly released Def Leppard

EP (copies of which were also on sale that night which included the song *'Getcha Rocks off'* [16])

Although we didn't know it then, around this time Def Leppard approached Frank to join the band as their permanent drummer. He turned it down opting to stay with the Next Band.

Def Leppard went on to become one of the biggest rock bands in the world selling more than 100 million records worldwide and in 2018 were inducted into the rock n' roll Hall of Fame.

The Next Band made no more recordings and split up the following year!

From time to time in life, we have crossroads moments where we are forced to make choices. Some of these choices are major at the time. Others don't seem that big then, but down the track turn out to be significant. Sometimes they turn out to be right choices, sometimes not.

I confess my heart goes out to Frank on this one. It's probably a decision that I would have made at that moment too. How do you handle those sorts of things when they happen? I guess the answer is you just have to press on. As Robbie Williams blatantly put it: *'No Regrets, they don't work'*. After all, who knows, maybe even the paths we choose at crossroads moments, even if they appear to be wrong, actually may be the right ones after all?

---

[16] **This track was reissued as the first single when they signed to Phonogram the following year. Following some Radio 1 promotion, it did well and became a springboard to many successes to follow.**

Talking of decisions you regret, I bought the Next Band's record that evening and still have it today. It brings back great memories. I thought about buying the Def Leppard EP, but in the end chose not to – after all /they were just the support band. Shame really, I've just checked 'Discogs' [17] and there's one copy for sale at £622.

---

[17] **Discogs.com: The best online music site for all recorded music, having one of the world's biggest databases. Great for collectors, buying and selling or anyone wanting to find out a band's discography**

Chapter 7. A Whole Lotta Waiting
Led Zeppelin
Knebworth – 1979

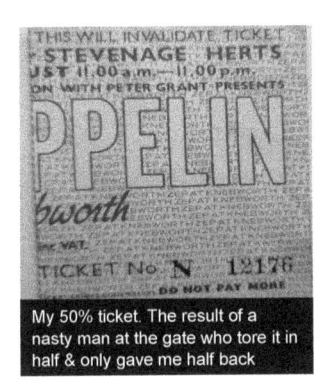

My 50% ticket. The result of a nasty man at the gate who tore it in half & only gave me half back

This gig took place on two consecutive Saturdays in August 1979. Our tickets were for the second week. We decided to drive down the day before due to the anticipated crowds. We parked the vehicle in a massive car park allocated for the festival and slept in the car overnight. Well, when I say 'slept' I mean I spent about four hours trying to attain a level of comfort that would induce sleep. Unfortunately, that never really happened. So, we ended up getting up at 3.30am and making our way to the entrance of Knebworth Park. The start time of the show was set for 11am yet surprisingly the gates were already open at 4am. Now you probably would assume that taking your place that early would ensure a place at the front. Well, you assume wrong. I simply couldn't believe how many people were already there, settled in for the long haul.

My overriding memory of this gig is taking our place at 4.15am, looking towards the stage and it seeming miles away. Then just before Led Zeppelin came onstage, turning around, and seeing an endless sea of people behind me stretching way beyond where the eye could see, and concluding that we <u>were</u> in fact near the front!!

It is still unknown what the attendance was for this festival. Police estimated up to 120,000 each week. I can easily believe that. It is certainly the biggest crowd I've ever been a part of.

Throngs at Knebworth. Somewhere there's a stage.

The festival line up was interesting in its uninterestingness. A band called 'The New Barbarians' were main support. This was in effect, The Rolling Stones without Jagger. Keith Richards and Ronnie Wood belted out some R.S. faves alongside new material that nobody was really interested in. It was all a bit 'Hey-ho'...which also summed up the other performers on the bill: Todd Rundgren, Southside Johnny & the Asbury Jukes, Commander Cody, and [believe it or not] openers Chas & Dave. Sadly, the most memorable thing about the line-up was the long waits in between each band.

By the time Led Zeppelin took the stage we had been in our position around eighteen hours. All discomfort was forgotten though, as we lapped up two and a half hours of classic rock, finishing with the beautiful and moving *'Stairway to Heaven'* with Robert Plant bathed in a rainbow backlight. I remember Jimmy Page performing a long guitar solo within a pyramid of green laser light. I also recall the encores were 'Rock and Roll' and 'Whole Lotta Love' with a further planned encore ditched as time was well past the curfew of midnight.

At the end we staggered out exhausted, and somehow eventually got out of the carpark and onto the A1, pulling into the first available layby, and crashing out – the discomfort of the car not registering an iota this time. We completed the journey home early the next morning.

This is one of those gigs which was tough to endure, yet looking back, one that has achieved iconic status, and I'm mighty pleased to have been there.

Fun Facts on Knebworth '79

- The largest stage ever constructed.
- Noise complaints from 7 miles away.
- 750 feet of urinals constructed.
- Nearby Tesco sold 75% of its stock.
- Sainsbury's reported the loss of 150 trolleys.
- The team of cleaners struggled to get the site ready for the second week
- Led Zepp's fee rumoured to be £1 million.
- The concert overran & Lord Cobbold (Knebworth's owner) ended up in Court.
- The gig received mixed reviews in the press, with some calling the Led Zepp's performance 'sluggish and rusty'.

Chapter 8. Bon Voyage
The Who
Wembley Stadium – 1979

Front rows DUCK! Roger Daltrey in fine Mic-swinging form

My first concert experience at Wembley Stadium and it was to see *'The Who'* reformed for the first time since the death of Keith Moon – former Faces drummer Kenny Jones filling in. The edge was still there; Daltrey with his curly mane cut short, was in fine mic swinging form, Townsend was leaping around with endless energy and Entwistle was... well, Entwistle – as solid as (and with as much personality as) a rock.

Starting the set with *'Substitute'* and finishing with the epic *'Won't get Fooled Again'*, this was a top set full of familiar Who classics

> THE EMPIRE STADIUM WEMBLEY
>
> Harvey Goldsmith by arrangement with Trinifold Ltd. presents
>
> No ticket genuine unless it carries a LIONS HEAD watermark below
>
> **The Who**
>
> and their friends
> See music press for other artists appearing
>
> SATURDAY 18 AUGUST 1979
> Gates open at 2.00 p.m.
>
> Tickets £8.00 inc. VAT in advance
> £8.50 inc. VAT on the day
>
> ENTER AT TURNSTILE
>
> **D**
>
> N°. 07972
>
> Free access throughout Stadium
> Licensed Bars. Do not bring bottles or cans.
> Ticket holders consent to the filming and sound recording of themselves as members of the audience.
>
> To be retained   See Plan and conditions on back

We managed to get near the front for this. It was a hot day I remember, but it didn't stop us both jumping around and standing around for hours on end, (more the latter).

The support line up of three artists was an interesting mix. First up was Nils Lofgren, Springsteen's guitarist who played a forgettable set. Next up were AC/DC followed by The Stranglers. It was criminal that the Stranglers got second billing. Their set was mostly unknown tracks off their new album strangely avoiding playing most of their previous hits. It was a lacklustre performance in all and they failed to win the crowd.

AC/DC on the other hand played a stormer. I had seen the Aussie Rockers in Derby the previous year and from that point on they became one of my favourite bands. The gimmick of vocalist Bon Scott carrying Angus Young, school boy guitarist on his shoulders through the audience during the track *'Rocker'* was repeated at Wembley. Needless to say, it took a little longer this time to get back on the stage. Bon was in fantastic form at Wembley. Little did I know that this would be the last time I would see him. Six months later, he was dead, having choked on his own vomit after a binge drinking session.

SUMMER OF '79

I was fortunate to see The Who again in 2024 at the Royal Albert Hall. Daltrey, aged eighty, still swung the mic, although perhaps not quite so far. Townsend, aged seventy-nine, wasn't jumping quite so high, yet still performed his 'windmill' guitar technique with the same enthusiasm. Overall, forty-five years on from the Wembley show, the power, energy, and charismatic presence of these two rock legends was still undeniably evident.

Chapter 9. The Freddie Gigs
Queen
1978-1984

I saw Queen with Freddie eight times. The first was at Earl's Court (Chapter 3) and the last time was Wembley Stadium (Chapter 33). The other in-between times were as follows:

1. Empire Pool Wembley 1978

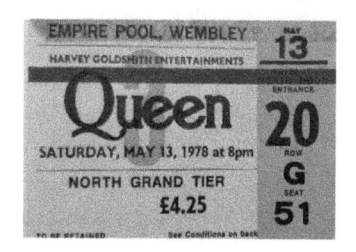

After the joy of Earl's Court, there was no way I was going to miss the next Queen tour. I didn't have to wait long; in fact, only eleven months!

The new album *'News of the World'* was released along with the announcement of a tour with the same name. This of course meant that for the first time the show ended with the two songs on the double A-sided single released from the album, namely: *'We Will Rock You'* and *'We are the Champions'*. This has never changed for any Queen tour to date, and why should it? Is there any better pair of live singalong anthems? I mean <u>EVER!?</u> Also, *WWRY* opened the show too, a ferocious rock version which worked as well as an opener as the original version did at the end.

What remains in my memory from this show is not so much Freddie, but drummer Roger Taylor, for two reasons.

Firstly, at the end of the gig he kicked over the drum kit and extensively spread it around the stage with his feet. I read later that he only ever did this a handful of times and usually when he was annoyed!

The second reason was that after the show we made our way to try and find an entrance/exit or 'stage door', where the band may come out. My memory is a bit hazy on this but we ended up outside some gates at the end of a driveway from the arena. After about fifteen minutes wait, some limos appeared coming towards us down the driveway. The gates were opened by security guards and I got the briefest of glimpses of Brian in the first car and Freddie in the second as they passed by. The third car pulled up right by us (waiting for the ones in front to move). The rear window was down and there in the back was Roger in between two stunning girls. Spontaneously, about half a dozen of us waiting, took a couple of steps up to the window. Roger said something like *'Hi Guys'* and extended his hand. I was about second in line and managed a quick handshake whilst at the same time uttering an imaginative reply...I think it was *"Good show Roger"*. Then the two cars in front moved and suddenly the drummer with his limo and contents therein - were gone. Slightly dazed we headed back to the tube when it suddenly occurred to me that I had no idea where John the bass player was. There may have been a fourth limo behind Roger's but I realised I'd never even noticed.

Finally, one aside on this venue. The 'Empire Pool' had existed since its opening in 1934. It was built originally for the Empire Games (held in that year) as a swimming/ ice skating facility. After forty four years, this gig was the last event at this venue under this name before it was officially re-branded (much more appropriately) as 'Wembley Arena'. [18]

2. Alexandra Palace 1979

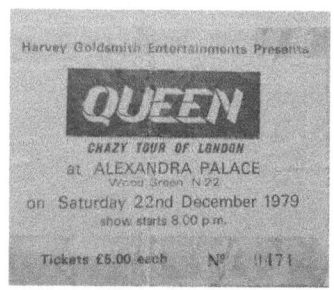

> Harvey Goldsmith Entertainments Presents
> **QUEEN**
> CRAZY TOUR OF LONDON
> at ALEXANDRA PALACE
> Wood Green N.22
> on Saturday 22nd December 1979
> show starts 8.00 p.m.
> Tickets £5.00 each   N° 0471

Queen were always up for something different and this time embarked on a short *'Crazy Tour of London'* in December, playing in unusual venues, such as the Lyceum ballroom and Purley Tiffany's club in Croydon. Tickets were impossible to get for the small venues so it was the Ally Pally, more by necessity than choice, where we ended up.

Alexandra Palace in North London, is located on a hill in the park of the same name. It is best known for its broadcasting history, with the BBC launching its first full TV service from here in 1936. It was also used for housing refugees in both World wars.

---

[18] **This became the SSE Arena in 2014 and from 2022 the OVO arena.**

Despite having the odd concert over the years (The Stones and Pink Floyd were a couple) it was not a common gig location so we arrived early, knowing little about it, other than it was an all-standing venue. It turned out to be a massive hall akin to an aircraft hangar interspersed with large pillars.

Three days before Christmas, our *"goodwill towards men"* was tested in queuing for two hours standing in snow and the freezing cold awaiting entry. When the doors did finally open, it was a rush to the front for another two hours waiting for the concert to start. Was it worth it? Oh my goodness, YES!.

This was the only time I got close to the front for a Freddie gig, and it was a memorable experience. Songs from the latest album *'Jazz'* got their first airing including *'Fat Bottomed Girls'* and *'Don't Stop me Now'*.[19]

Ally Pally – one of those hands could be mine

I don't think the sound was at its best in the venue, but when you're at the front, this matters less. It was a magnificent gig, a wild extravagant party, an immer-

---

[19] **The setlist was pretty much the one featured on the 'Live Killers' double album.**

sive celebration. I mean who could ever forget Freddie's appearance for WWRY wearing as a reprise the silver one-piece glitter leotard whilst perched on the shoulders of a huge bruising body builder dressed in a *Superman* outfit. Now Christmases don't get much better than that!

3. Wembley Arena 1980

One year later we were back at Wembley Arena for *'The Game'* tour. The overriding memory of this gig was the breaking news of John Lennon's death. We had heard on the way to the concert that he has been shot, and on arrival at Wembley there was a strange 'hush' in the air, as people were struggling to comprehend the loss to the music world. It must have been difficult for the band to go on stage but they responded in the best way possible. After the gentle *'Love of my Life',* Freddie sang a beautiful version of *'Imagine'* with such tender emotion, there wasn't a dry eye in the house. A moving special moment!

4. Milton Keynes Bowl 1981

My only festival experience of Queen, and a gig that silenced the critics. The band had come under a barrage of negativity, particularly from the media, following the release of their tenth studio album 'Hot Space' which had a dominant funk/ disco feel. Freddie, on introducing one of the songs from the album, commented 'I don't know what all the fuss is about, it's only a f*#^*g record!'. Any question of a retreat from being predominantly a rock band, was soundly put to sleep. For a start, they arrived in a 'Queen' logoed helicopter flying over the crowd (how rock and roll is that?). The band then performed a blistering set; one that can be fully enjoyed on the officially released DVD/BluRay 'Queen on Fire - Live at the Bowl'. Incidentally, support bands for this gig were 'Joan Jett', 'Heart' and strangely 'The Teardrop Explodes', a psychedelic post punk outfit led by singer Julian Cope, who got canned off well before their set ended.

5. NEC Birmingham 1984
and
6. Wembley Arena 1984

Two shows in one week for me. This 1984 tour promoted the new album 'The Works' and the stage design was based on a scene from Fritz Lang's 'Metropolis' which featured rotating cog-wheels at the rear of the stage. This linked with the video from the album's opening track and first single *'Radio Ga Ga'*.

Queen's back catalogue was now at the stage of being able to produce non-stop hits, which they did. Yet there were still new classics emerging – the crowd participation of *'Radio Ga Ga'* and the brilliant *'I want to Break Free'* which saw Freddie strut on stage with a massive pair of false breasts (instantly recognisable from the hilarious video accompanying the single release – a parody of 'Coronation Street' with each band member playing a character). Also, to please hardcore fans, a number of songs from the early albums were introduced back to the set: *'Keep Yourself Alive'*, *'Liar'* and *'Great King Rat'* (from debut album Queen), *'Seven Seas of Rhye'* (from Queen 2) and *'Now I'm here'*,

'Stone Cold Crazy' and 'Killer Queen' (from third record 'Sheer Heart Attack').

It was interesting seeing the band play twice in a week. The first was at the NEC Birmingham. I actually went with my Mum to this gig. She really wanted to go. This shows the diversity both of Queen's appeal and my gig going companions! However, for the first time the sound was not quite as perfect as the other previous arena gigs I'd been to. Also, Freddie seemed very tired at times, a couple of times leaning on his piano and taking a breather. So, this wasn't the best Queen show.

The second gig however was back at Wembley Arena and the last night of the UK leg. This was a stunning concert; Freddie was so much more energised, the band connecting better and producing a memorable night.

Queen were now widely recognised as one of the top bands globally, and it dawned on me that I was seeing not only one of the best live bands ever, but one of the best frontmen / performers. I knew I would continue to go to their gigs every time they toured.

Little did I know I would only see Queen with Freddie one more time!

PART TWO
THE 1980s

Chapter 10 – Taking up Residency
The Hammersmith Gigs
Hammersmith Odeon 1980

In Sept 1979 I embarked on a three-year degree course in Estate Management at Kingston Upon Thames Polytechnic, [20] South West London.

I was always taught to make the most of opportunities and by the start of term two (also the start of the 1980s), I certainly did. I have to admit though that this was nothing to do with my course. It was by utilising the proximity of one of London's most popular gig venues, the Hammersmith Odeon.

1980 became my most prolific year of gig going, which included twelve concerts in one year at this iconic venue alone. I confess it seemed like I'd almost taken up residency status there.

So here goes:

---

[20] This became Kingston University the year after I'd finished. I'd like to think I was partially responsible for this prestigious promotion in title. Sadly, we all know different!

1. Blondie

Blondie were a band that broke free from the fringe punk/ new wave label they had fallen in to, successfully crossing over into the mainstream. As I see it, this was down to two reasons.

Debbie Harry wearing something resembling THE Skirt

Firstly, through a string of great songs released as successful singles. Secondly, the sex appeal of singer, Debbie Harry, whose bleached blonde hair, dark eyeliner and ripped clothing, got many a heart beating to a precariously rapid rhythm. Now which of the two, do you think, was the reason for several of my friends being keen on getting a ticket?

Such was the demand for this gig that it rapidly sold out and a second night added. As a result, some of us got tickets for the first night and others for the second night.

My ticket was for the first night, and it turned out to be a brilliant gig. Starting with *'Dreaming'*, the setlist included a cover of Bowie's *'Heroes'* plus all the Blondie classic hits including *'Atomic'*, *'Hanging on the Telephone'*, *'Heart of Glass'* and *'One Way or Another'* to close.

Two things were the talking point of the evening: first (by far) was the sexy leather skirt Debbie Harry wore, that left little to the imagination. Second was the drummer, Clem Burke, who was simply breath-taking in his performance[21], and still today is one of the best drummers I have ever seen.

After our gig we reported back to those who had landed tickets for the following night, especially emphasising the treat they were in for with DH's outfit.

It goes without saying that there was severe leg pulling after the report came back from the 'second-nighters', who whilst raving how good the gig had been, admitted that Debbie had worn a rather boring trouser suit for their show!

2. Barclay James Harvest

A college mate got me into Barclay James Harvest (fondly abbreviated to BJH) a soft pop-rock band. They had the unusual attribute of two front men who sung on their own compositions. For me, their earlier work released in the 1970s far outstrips the later material, and 'Live Tapes' a double live album from 1978 captures the band at their very best.

BJH - Doing what they do best?

A few months after this gig BJH played a free concert in front of the Reichstag in West Berlin, with an estimated attendance of 250,000, and it is for this event they are best known.

---

[21] Clem Burke is still Blondie's drummer [at the time of writing] and is the only other original member alongside Debbie Harry.

This gig at H.O. was disappointing with the band choosing to play mostly new songs and omitting classic oldies. Also, I discovered BJH are not a charismatic band live – they stood and played their songs, encouraging audience participation only in the encore, 'Hymn'

I saw BJH again twelve years later in 1992, a much better setlist including early classics. But it re-affirmed my opinion that they are a better recorded band than live (as some bands simply are). It's ironic that they are best known for a live show and their best album is a live one. However, my advice should you feel the urge to check out BJH, would be to invest in a copy of 'Live Tapes.'

3. Wishbone Ash

They don't come much more a classic stereotype rock band than Wishbone Ash. Catchy solid songs and great guitar solos. I've seen them three or four times over the years, and whilst they're never going to be in the realms of 'best gigs ever', I've never been disappointed and always enjoyed a good night out.

4. UFO

Here we go again. Bigger venue this time, and the usual high-class concert. First part of show featured tracks off the new album 'No Place to Run' and the second non-stop classics. Pete Way, the bassist, was on top form, as was vocalist Phil Mogg. No Schenker though!

5. Peter Gabriel

There's one thing you can usually say about Peter Gabriel – expect the unexpected. I mean who would call a tour *'The Tour of China 1984'* when it was actually 1980 and no shows on the tour were in China? [22] This unpredictable concert from the ex-Genesis vocalist, started in a slightly unsettling manner with Gabriel & his band coming through the audience dressed in black jumpsuits to a track called *'Intruder.'* Each member carried a torch and shone the beams on members of the audience as they passed by!

Most of the set came from the new third album, called *'Peter Gabriel'* (which incidentally was also the title of his first two albums!) His best-known song, *'Solsbury Hill'*, came early in the set, and there were no Genesis songs performed. A great if not unorthodox ending was a solo piano version of *'Here Comes the Flood'*.

This gig kind of messed with my mind from the point of view that as I made my journey home, my ponderings were trying to decide how I felt about the show and actually whether I'd enjoyed it or not... and the thing is I really couldn't decide!

Maybe that was exactly the reaction Gabriel was aiming for.

---

[22] The 'Tour of China 1984' "programme" for this gig consisted of a 6"x 4" 90-page red book. This echoed Chairman Mau's "Little Red Book" outlining his communist regime in the form of quotations. The whole theme appears to be a jibe at the Chinese government, whilst at the same time giving a nod to George Orwell's prophetic novel.

6. Pat Travers

"PT's playing, Rockin' this lazy town." [23]

Artists who toured the UK often liked to finish at the Hammersmith Odeon, because of the iconic nature of the venue. For the artist, it was often viewed as a 'flagship' gig and often resulted in them pulling something a little extra out of the bag.

This made it interesting because one thing about attending the Hammersmith Odeon so frequently was that on entry you passed the box office and they always had a list of new shows just announced. How dangerous is that!? So, on more than one occasion I left the show with a ticket in my pocket for the next one. That's how I got second row tickets to Pat Travers.

Got to love Pat Travers! This blues rock guitarist from Canada came on the scene in the mid-70s and got my attention through the release of a brilliant album called *'Makin' Magic.'*

I had seen PT and his band at the Nottingham Playhouse in the '70s and like the UFO gig (c/f chapter 5), it was spoilt by the formal venue and its protocol. But this show itself was fantastic. PT gave it his all; combining that with a ground floor second row seat, you couldn't fail to be in the moment. The result was one electric night. Magic was made!

---

[23] **Lyrics from *'Rock n' Roll Susie'*, a track from Pat Travers *'Makin' Magic'* album released on Polydor records 1977**

7. *Genesis*

The first of several times I saw Genesis. They were a band you either loved or hated. I came to love them and they have remained one of my favourite bands through the years of my life. This gig was the *'Duke'* tour (one of the best Genesis albums in my view). I also saw them on the *'Abacab'* tour in '82 (see Chapter 23), once in '84 promoting the new album imaginatively called *'Genesis'* and finally at Wembley Stadium in '87 on the *'Invisible Touch'* tour.

8. Sammy Hagar

Dynamic rocker Sammy Hagar has had a highly successful career as a solo artist as well as with several different bands including *'Montrose'* and *'Van Halen'*. He has legendary status in the US, having been inducted into the *'Rock n' Roll Hall of Fame'* in 2007. In 2022 he turned seventy-five and got rave reviews for his new album released that year with his current band *'The Circle'*.

This gig at the Odeon back in 1980, was at the height of his solo era. What I remember most about this gig was Hagar's outfit - a bright red leather number. This was all part of an obsession with the colour, e.g. one song being called *'Red'* and his records being released on red vinyl.

The other thing I recall was that it was deafening. From memory probably the loudest concert I have ever been to. It was a wild, raucous, 'let your hair down', night of rock during which Hagar played most of the then newly released (and brilliant) live album appropriately titled '*Loud and Clear*'.

Well, half of the title was certainly true!

9. Thin Lizzy

A band and gig I consider fortunate to have seen. Soaring in popularity and confidence following the success of the outstanding '*Live & Dangerous*' double live album. Lizzy were always a live band first and foremost. This gig proved the point, rocking through '*Jailbreak*' '*Rosalie*' & '*The Boys are back in Town*' among others.

Vocalist and bassist, Phil Lynott, compellingly occupied centre stage and it was like the band played around him with a tight synergy. There were moments of raw power, aggression and fun as well as some delicate and sensitive touches.

One such poignant moment was Lynott singing the words '*I've got to give it up*' repeatedly in a haunting soulful way as an intro to this song about addiction. In hindsight, it took on more power following Lynott's tragic death in 1986 due to heroin/drug abuse.

This concert was actually released for streaming in 2020 under the title '*Hammersmith Live 1980*'.

10. Rush

No support - just a two and a half hour high intensity set from this Canadian three-piece band who had by now, built a huge following worldwide. They had been together since 1968, plenty of time to practice becoming a tight outfit - and tight they were! Opening with the twenty minute epic song '2112', the band drove full tilt through most of their classic tracks, where simple songs such as *'Closer to the Heart'*, *'Spirit of Radio'* and *'Working Man'* sat alongside more complex prog rock tracks such as *'Xanadu'* and *'Hemispheres'*.

One notable thing about this gig was the size of drummer Neil Peart's kit. It took up half the stage, and worthy of closing the set with a stunning drum solo! [24] [c/f appendix A:9]

This was a hot June night and I was knackered well before the encore. Yet the energy and adrenalin of the band carried through until the final raucous riff. A great show!

These ten gigs all occurred in the first half of the year. The remaining two at the Hammy Odeon deserve their own chapter.

---

[24] How many other bands finish their set with a drum solo? But then how many bands have a drum kit the size of Heathrow?

Chapter 11 – High Voltage Rock n' Roll
AC/DC
Hammersmith Odeon & The Apollo Victoria 1980

Three times in one week may seem a bit extravagant to see the same band, but the fact that AC/DC were one of my favourites is not the only reason for this over-indulgence.

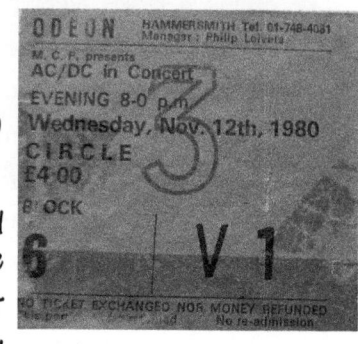

Firstly, due to my prolificness in gig going, I had established a bit of a reputation as the person with 'know-how' on getting tickets for gigs. So, I started to get approached by others to get tickets for them. When the AC/DC tour was announced, a few of my friends, knowing I would be going, put in requests. However, there were two problems that arose. One was that there was huge demand for tickets, particularly as this was singer Brian Johnson's first tour as Bon Scott's replacement. Secondly, not all my friends could go on the same night. So, I ended up getting odd pairs of tickets on different nights at the Hammy Odeon and also at the Apollo, Victoria (the latter venue added when the former sold out). Anyway, due to mix-ups and back outs, I ended up at three shows.

But let's answer the question as to why I liked this band so much at this time.

I think, on trying to break it down, that you have all the elements that combine to make 'rock n' roll' great, but in a very simple formulaic way:

Basic powerful riffs ± cheeky catchy lyrics ± great guitar work ± incredible high voltage energy ± infectious tongue in cheek fun ± a unique and unforgettable gimmick.

The latter took the form of guitarist Angus Young as a naughty out of control schoolboy [25] whose escapades on stage during a gig always provide plenty of humorous surprises!

In summary the package the band offered was a complete entertainment spectacle! You couldn't help but like them; in fact, you couldn't help but love them!

So on with the show(s)!

What a great start. The house lights go out, and from high up above the stage descends a massive brass bell with the band logo brazened on it. It's agonisingly slow but serves to build the anticipation. Once at stage level it stops. On runs Brian Johnson to rapturous applause and tolls the bell. From the speakers blast the opening riff from the first track off the new *'Back in Black'* record, *'Hells Bells'*, and on struts Angus in full uniform, cap and satchel - and we're away.

All the songs we wanted to hear kept coming, from the new single *'You Shook me all night Long'* to the older faves, *'High Voltage'*, *'Whole Lotta Rosie'* and *'Let there be Rock'* as a final encore. There was a great

---

[25] **Of course, as the years pass by and the band age, this becomes more ludicrously funny.**

moment when Angus does a lengthy striptease, removing jacket, tie and shirt with a teasing suggestion of his shorts to follow. Thankfully, a quick moon on top of a speaker ended the routine and brought the biggest cheer of the night.

After my final show at the Apollo, my friend and I waited at the stage door for possible autographs. After some time we realised there were two stage doors and the band had exited through the other one, some time ago!

Ah well, you can't win them all!

Chapter 12– Mud Glorious Mud
The Police
Milton Keynes Bowl 1980

The overriding memory of this event was the mud. Thunderstorms were rife both before and during the day, and things were messy!

This one-day festival was called *'Rockatta de Bowl'*, a play on the Police's second album release *'Regatta de Blanc'*. A review in a music mag post event had a headline suggesting a more appropriate name: *'Mudflatta de Bowl'*.

Although we did our best (with some success) to stay out of the main swamp areas, make no mistake, we were distinctive shades of brown by the end.

Tom Robinson, Squeeze (with Jools Holland on keyboards) and reggae outfit UB40 provided good support but it wasn't until The Police, led by Sting hit the stage that the mud was finally forgotten and we sang and danced through a brilliant set.

But it was the mud that had the final say and provided the most unforgettable memory of the day, which bizarrely involved returning to our car after the gig!

The car parks were basically a series of fields, each field having one exit. The organisers it seemed, had not thought this through, failing to consider what may happen when you add the combination of heavy traffic and heavy rain to a grass field. The result, as any reasonable person would hazard a guess at, is a complete quagmire!

And so it was. By the time we had found the correct carpark and then our car, bedlam had ensued with vehicles galore already stuck deep in the mud, totally blocking the exit. It was complete chaos!

But just when some tempers were starting to overheat, something extraordinary happened. In one of the most unselfish, giving acts I have ever witnessed, a group of five or six guys, who were simply gig goers, not officials, semi stripped to preserve their clothes and pushed every single car out of the car park – one by one, including ours. They coordinated and managed a complete escape for everyone in our field, and with a great attitude, laughing and singing through it all. So basically, when it was our turn, we had to drive right into the mud bath and then they pushed us out the other side.

I don't know who those guys were that day but from time to time over the last quarter of a century, when I have recalled this moment, I always breath a silent prayer of thanksgiving for that sacrificial act.

Chapter 13 – The Wall
Pink Floyd
Earls Court 1980

It had been three years since the monumental Queen gig, and for the first time since then I was back at this gigantic aircraft hangar of a venue. And no doubt about it, every centimetre was needed for Pink Floyd's performance of *'The Wall'*.

Now I have to confess that at the time of attending this gig, I wasn't a huge PF fan. It wasn't that I disliked them, I just hadn't got into their music that much. I knew *'Wish You were Here'* but had only heard snippets of their other albums. So when I went to Earl's Court, I'd only heard parts of *'the Wall'* album and really only knew the single *'Another Brick in the Wall part 2'*.

Looking back, I am fully aware I had no idea at the time what a brilliant work of art this album was, and I failed to appreciate the musical genius performed that evening. Despite that, I still recall having a sense that this was in some way an important gig, and that it was great to be there.

In hindsight of course it is easy to see why. Firstly, this was the last tour featuring the classic Floyd line up of Waters/ Gilmour/ Mason/ Wright.

Secondly, this was a ground-breaking show both in design and scale as well as audibly and visually.

Every cloud has a silver lining they say and so perhaps in this case, a benefit of not being that familiar with the music was that I naturally focused on the show. So here are my top ten memories of this unforgettable night (in reverse order).

10. THE CONSTRUCTION - During the whole first half as the band played, a team of people/roadies built the wall in blocks slowly, in front of the band. The last brick was placed on the very last note of *'Goodbye Cruel World'*, blocking out the band and bringing the show to the half time interval.

9. THE IMAGES - The harrowing pictures and cine-film of war scenes shown on the backing screen during some songs.

8. THE FLICKERING TV - Roger Waters in front of the completed wall singing *'Nobody Home'*, while sitting in an armchair watching a flickering TV.

7. THE PIG - A huge inflatable black pig floating over the audience!

6. THE DEMOLITION – The collapsing of the wall towards the end, when a huge explosion was followed by all the 'bricks' falling. I joined the rest of Earl's Court in being unable to discern whether a stunned silence or rapturous applause was more appropriate. The latter won through eventually.

5. THE FINISH – In an almost anticlimactic but brilliant ending, as the final down beat song *'Outside the Wall'* ended, Roger Waters picked up a clarinet and in a kind of 'pied piper' style, led the rest of the band off the stage.

4. THE REACTION - The sheer length of the thunderous applause of the crowd at the end of the performance. I thought we'd never get home!

3. THE TEACHER - A huge puppet of the teacher (replicated from the *'Another Brick pt 2'* video) who during the song towered above the crowd moving around with his spotlight eyes picking out individual audience members. Slightly unsettling!

2. THE PLANE - Right at the start, a large model aeroplane flying the full length of Earls Court, from the back, over the heads of the audience and crashing into the stage.

And No 1 – The Best Memory – THE SOLO OF SOLOS - I will never ever forget Dave Gilmour slowly rising into view above the completed wall, bathed in a backdrop of searing white lights amidst a sea of dry ice, playing an extended version of the magnificent guitar solo of *'Comfortably Numb'*. Words cannot describe that moment!

I came away at the end, feeling not only that I had seen something special but that I had been a part of

something special, and dare I say, in some strange way
– a part of musical history.

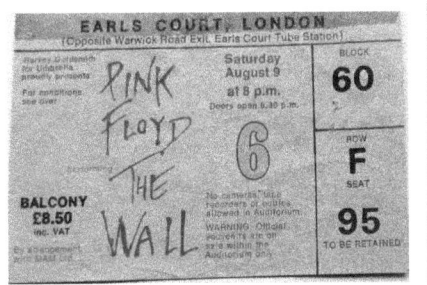

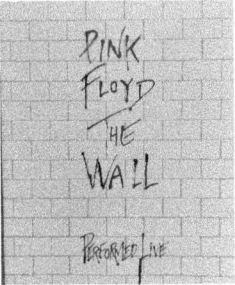

Chapter 14 – Long Live Rock n' Roll

Monsters of Rock 1

Castle Donington 1980

For the last twenty years plus, Donington Park near Nottingham has hosted the *'Download'* festival which has become the flagship event for the heavy rock/metal scene.

However, the roots of *'Download'* lay in its predecessor, *'The Monsters of Rock'* festival.

I was at the very first one, with headliners Rainbow, led by former Deep Purple virtuoso guitarist Richie Blackmore, along with Roger Glover on bass and Don Airey on keys (also Deep Purple), drummer Cozy Powell and new vocalist, Graham Bonnet.

I had got into Rainbow big time through their first four records, three excellent studio albums and one live double album. The vocalist for all these was Ronnie James Dio, a fine singer with a deep guttural powerhouse voice, and an impressive vocal range but due to "creative differences" with Blackmore,[26] had recently left the band.

I confess this did take the shine off my enthusiasm approaching the gig – how would Rainbow function without Dio?

I needn't have worried – this turned out to be a triumphant, no holds barred, show.

---

[26] I did end up seeing Dio sing live at the Hammersmith Odeon on New Year's eve 1992 when he fronted Black Sabbath. I went not because I liked BS, but I really wanted to see Ronnie sing live.

There was a healthy line up of bands on the bill. Judas Priest were the main support with singer Rob Halford in leather attire making an entrance on a Harley. The best of the rest was probably Barnsley Band Saxon, winning the crowd over with *anthems* *'Wheels of Steel' and '747 Strangers in the Night'*. German band The Scorpions were average, U.S. outfit April Wine poor, and Riot (who I had seen support Sammy Hagar earlier in the year) did well for an early daytime slot.

But with descending darkness came *Rainbow* and a memorable opening.

A dramatic classical music introduction gave way to a countdown on the big screen. At 'zero' an ear-splitting crowd cheer was interrupted over the PA by the voice of Judy Garland from the film, *'The Wizard of OZ'*: *"we're not in Kansas anymore. We must be over the rainbow…'* …
And then the stage erupted in a cacophony of explosions, smoke bombs, dry ice and fireworks as the band hit the stage. Suddenly we weren't in Kansas anymore! It was a stunning start!

I read subsequently that Richie Blackmore had announced prior to Donington that he had wanted to create something spectacularly special for this gig. The uncharacteristic nature of this announcement [27] got the rumour wheels turning:

---

[27] **Blackmore had a reputation of being a bit of a grumpy old misery, who never interacted with the press and was often accused of short changing the fans. For example, he was known for not believing in (and hence not playing) encores.**

Maybe Ritchie wanted to give the 60,000+ crowd paying £7.50 a bit more value for money than his reputation had established.

OR...

Maybe Richie simply wanted to celebrate being headliners at this first 'Monsters of Rock' festival of its kind?

OR....

Maybe *Rainbow* were 'going out with a bang'; this being their last ever gig as rumours were rife that Richie had a cunning plan to re-form *Deep Purple* [28]

OR....

Maybe Ritchie was just winding everybody up and simply generating publicity?

Whatever the intention was, he certainly fulfilled his promise.

In fact, at a dress rehearsal the previous day, a pile of gelignite was added to the special effects. The resultant bang was heard fifty miles away, blew twenty two of the PA's base speakers, knocked people off chairs and impaired the hearing of a supervisory police officer. Needless to say, the special effects were

---

[28] **Actually, this didn't happen until 1984**

toned down to something fractionally less apocalyptic for the actual show.

Rainbow's setlist turned out to be fantastic. It still contained several of Richie's ultra-L-O-N-G guitar solos but Graham Bonnet, despite looking more dressed for a disco than a hard rock gig, gave it his all. There was a memorable version of *'Stargazer'* and believe it or not, an encore! The show finished with Blackmore smashing his guitar to pieces and ramming its battered remains into an amp which promptly exploded and started belching flames. At the same time, thousands of fireworks lit the sky in what turned out to be an amazing display.

[Today we are used to spectacular fireworks on New Year's eve and indeed to close many stadium rock shows – but this was before all that and I for one had never seen anything like it].

We left with the final song ringing in our ears: *'Long Live Rock n' Roll'* and after this gig, we all could freely shout a loud 'Amen' to that.

Chapter 15 – Can you Hear me at the Back?
Rod Stewart
Wembley Arena 1980

This was Rod's *'Stupid Behaviour'* tour *[What do you mean you thought they all were?]*. This gig was a strange one. I knew when I got my ticket that the seat wasn't a good one, being located in the West Terrace, which is the opposite end of Wembley Arena to the stage. At least it was row 'P' so it wasn't right at the back, right? And it was seat 4 so it wasn't right at the end, right?

Wrong! It appears this was a crafty ploy by the Arena management to avoid you giving up all hope before the gig. Because I was in fact, on the very back row in the very end corner seat. There was no one behind me in the entire arena.

A few months earlier I had been to a superb play in the West End starring Peter Barkworth and Hannah Gordon. It started with the main character on stage looking out over the audience and addressing us with the line *'Can you hear me at the back?'* (the title of the play).

There were times in this gig I felt like yelling out *'Can you hear me at the front? I'm here at the back'* because I did feel a bit detached from the whole thing. It was like I was fighting to become part of things the whole way through.

Having said that, it was a fun show and who could fail not to sing along to the likes of 'Maggie May', 'Sailing' and the outrageous 'Do you think I'm sexy?'

Enjoyable - but from a distance!

Chapter 16 – U Who?
My Biggest Gig Mistake
Oct 11 1980

At Kingston, one of the frequent places of occupation was the Student Union Bar. If you ever wanted to find somebody, this was usually your first port of call (even at lecture time!). Indeed, many a fine hour was frittered away in the good old S.U. Bar.

Just off from the bar area was a separate self-contained room for live music that included a small one step off the ground stage area and standing room for perhaps two hundred people. Kingston would never stand out in anyone's memory for being the hot seat for gigs. The town had no concert venues of notable worth at that time so any bands that did play there tended to play at the Polytechnic.

I was surprised to see looking back, that the Poly had hosted some significant bands in its gig history. Pink Floyd played there in 1967, Elton John and Yes in 1971, Genesis and Bowie in 1972 and Motorhead in 1976.

There were only a few bands that I can recall seeing at the Union Bar during my time there. The first was Eddie and the Hot Rods, a new wave rock band who had one big chart hit with *'Do anything you want to Do'*. Others were Wishbone Ash who played a stormer, The Pirates, providing a wild night of rock n' roll and Manfred Mann's Earth Band who provided a great singalong night. I know I went to several more but my memory was no doubt affected by the cheap price of the beers the SU provided.

However, one evening is firmly lodged in my memory. Earlier in the day, I had met a friend who had told me there was a band playing in the Union bar that evening. *"Supposed to be a really exciting band – getting rave reviews - you on?".*

"Sure, sounds great, I'll meet you in the bar later" I replied.

That night the SU bar seemed to be quite full but a few of us managed to get a table and ordered in some drinks. Soon we were laughing and knocking back the beers. Around about 8.30pm, the guy I'd met earlier stands up – *'Time to go through, its about to start'* he announced. Half of the table got up to go. Some of us there, including me still had full glasses. *"We'll just finish these - You head on through we'll follow on'*

Of course, we had every intention of going in to see the band but somehow or other we got distracted - some other friends turned up and joined us, and conversation was flowing. About an hour later when we suddenly became aware of the time, we realised we had missed the start. So we decided to stay put, shrugged it off with a 'never mind there'll be plenty of other nights...', and with little thought, we carried on our conversation.

Around 10.30pm, I looked up from my table to see my friend standing there wide-eyed. I started to apologise for not going in but he cut through my attempts to speak.

'Oh my God' He said, 'that was one wild night, I think I have just seen the best band ever'

'Really,' I said 'That good?'

'Unbelievable'. 'Absolutely incredible'.

'Who were they again?' I asked

His reply which meant nothing on the night, but now and for the rest of my days will be forever be seared in my mind: 'They were called U2'.

Chapter 17 - A Tonic for the Troops
The Boomtown Rats
Hammersmith Odeon 1981

A slight diversion from my usual choice of gigs, but a thoroughly enjoyable one.

The Boomtown Rats were another of those bands that managed to escape the punk label and move into the advancing new wave rock era. They did this largely with a couple of great, different and imaginative singles: *'Rat Trap'* and the slightly disturbing *'I don't like Mondays'* (which was the response of a 16-year-old girl when asked why she had gone on a shooting rampage in her school.) Both of these songs took on a new dimension live and were worth the ticket money alone.

This was Bob Geldof long before *Live Aid* and a knighthood, who then was known as simply an unorthodox frontman and partner of TV presenter Paula Yates. (Not necessarily in that order).

The band were on fire and Geldof was in good voice, pushing the boundaries with his own unique style of performing.[29] It was also good to see Johnny Fingers the keyboard/ pianist wearing his pyjamas on stage. (I thought it was just for the videos).

All in all, a fun night and in line with the name of the Rats' latest album – it was a Tonic for the Troops.

---

[29] **His style once described in a review in the Guardian Newspaper as** *'a dancing, prancing, restless mess of a frontman'*.

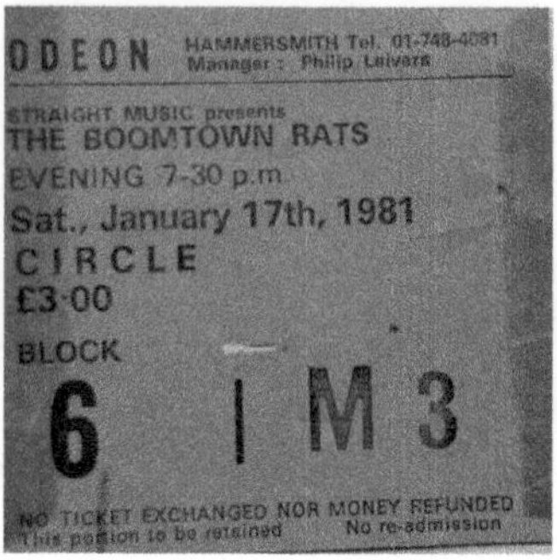
ODEON HAMMERSMITH Tel. 01-748-4081
Manager : Philip Leivers
STRAIGHT MUSIC presents
THE BOOMTOWN RATS
EVENING 7-30 p.m.
Sat., January 17th, 1981
CIRCLE
£3·00
BLOCK
6 I M 3
NO TICKET EXCHANGED NOR MONEY REFUNDED
This portion to be retained No re-admission

The Boomtown Rats

Chapter 18 – Long Way from Home
Whitesnake
Hammersmith Odeon 1981

Of all the gigs I have ever been to, this stands out as the one with the best atmosphere. Most gigs have a build up with a bit of clapping and cheering beforehand, which tends to crescendo as the band come on stage. Not this one! I have never heard such prolonged noise, chanting, singing, clapping, stomping – a massive ongoing noise. It was incredible. Why this gig? Why this band? I don't know!

Whitesnake are another band like Rainbow with Deep Purple connections. Singer, David Coverdale, left DP in 1978 and formed Whitesnake. Whilst popular in the UK, it wasn't until the late 1980s that they achieved success in the U.S. which took their following to another level. Their music is often described as *'Rock Blues'* – Coverdale's voice certainly has a bluesy, earthy tone and when he adds in some raunchy grunts and groans, it all comes together very well, fitting nicely with the often somewhat suggestive lyrics.

One of my flatmates attended this gig with me because of one song called *'Long Way from Home'*, the opening track off Whitesnake's 1979 album, 'Love hunter'.

She loved that track and made it clear the only reason she was going was because of this one song. [30] *"They better play it"*, she kept saying to me in the weeks leading up to the gig. I had my doubts as it wasn't a major hit and there had been a further two albums released since then as well as a new one to promote, waiting in the wings.

Did that deter her? Not a bit. During the gig after every song played, despite my cringing, my flatmate yelled at the top of her voice, "*PLAY 'LONG WAY FROM HOME'*". But her screaming pleas seemed to attract little attention being swallowed up in the vast ocean of noise.

'When the band took the stage for the encore, David Coverdale basked in the rapturous response before stepping up to the microphone. 'Tonight, we're going to do something a little different. We're going to play something we don't normally play these days. But there's a girl out there whose been shouting for this song, so tonight I dedicate to her...'Long Way from Home'.

Ahhh, wouldn't that have been the perfect ending to the evening? Unfortunately, it didn't happen like that. *'Long Way from Home'* wasn't played at all during the gig.

Afterwards when we stepped out onto the street, the quietness was notable – it was London with its usual traffic, but it seemed a calm serenity after the

---

[30] **However, I think a close second was that she fancied Coverdale rotten, with his long flowing locks and his sexy grunts. [Her words not mine]**

tumult of the gig. Neither of us spoke for a while. I was just about to semi-apologise that ~~THE~~ song hadn't been played, when my companion gave a sigh and said in an almost dream-like way *'Wow, wasn't that the best night ever?!*

Chapter 19 – Let There Be Rock
Monsters of Rock 2
Donington Park 1981

The success of last year's event ensured a second 'Monsters of Rock' Festival. It was not only the fact that AC/DC were down to top the bill but also the strength of the support line up, that confirmed a return for me. And it obviously wasn't just me – but 65,000 others turned up, not far off twice the numbers of last year. This made things somewhat challenging in a number of ways.

Firstly, the toilets seemed to have deteriorated in quality. This year they consisted of a series of scaffold poles with canvas sheets slung between them with the considerable amount of contents emptying into a large hole in the ground. As a small concession to health and safety there was a piece of rope alongside to 'stop' you falling in.

Secondly, the 'missileing'. In between bands just for something to do, some people started to throw things to another part of the crowd. This seemed to catch on and before you knew it, everybody decided to throw anything and everything into the air at various angles and directions. Before long, the sky became a flowing ocean of toilet rolls, chicken legs, banana skins, paper aeroplanes, half eaten sandwiches and plastic bottles full of liquid. This takes on a different dimension when you know that for one reason or another (and I'm sure the general state the toilets were in was a key factor) people were resorting to peeing in the plastic drink containers, putting the cap on very loosely and flinging it over the crowd, so the cap came off mid-flight! [31]

It was amazing to see AC/DC again, this time at an outdoor festival. In many ways they played it safe, pretty much sticking to the same setlist as last year.

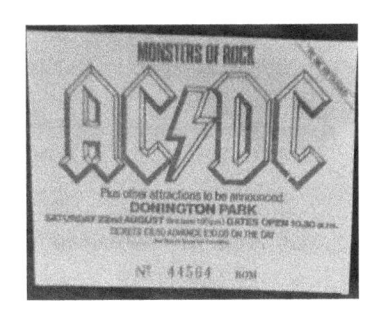

Of course, they were the best band and so they should have been, with the fireworks, light show and the acceptance now of Brian Johnson as replacement to Bon Scott - but only just.

Slade (with original line up) were a close second. I guess it was a gamble for the promoters to include a 70s band who had kind of lost popularity, but suddenly

---

[31] **Why is it when you're young, these things don't bother you at all, but when you get older, you writhe on the ground even at the thought of it?**

found a new lease of life. And they cracked it. They played their set in daylight and got the crowd well and truly going with a combination of some of their heavier rock material and classic singalongs. ("*So here it is Merry Christmas*"... in August?)

Then there was Blackfoot – an underrated Southern US Rock band in the style of Lynyrd Skynyrd complete with '*Highway Song*', their own '*Freebird*'. They were great despite the early daytime slot. I saw them headline in Leicester the following year and they were truly amazing. ['*Marauder*' is still one of the best rock albums of all time in my opinion].

The main support was Whitesnake, who did a slightly abridged set from the one I'd seen at the Hammy Odeon three months earlier. Coverdale, with all his experience along with the tight band, made them look very comfortable and in command on the bigger stage. They pulled it off big time and were rewarded two years later when asked to headline the fourth MOR Festival.

The worst band of the day were 'Blue Oyster Cult', who most people knew for '*Don't fear the Reaper*' and nothing else. I'm not sure why but the sound played up during their set plus I later discovered their drummer went AWOL the day before and a stand-in had to battle through. Didn't matter, the sound was bad anyway!

Thinking back I remember only good things about this gig. Apparently, it rained a lot. I have no memory of that - nor do I recall being hit by any missile or of even going to the toilet although I must have done.

But for some reason I do remember Noddy Holder yelling out to 65,000 fans in a field in mid-summer: 'It's CHRISTMASSSS'

Slade: festive summer fun!

Chapter 20 – A legendary Venue
Magnum
The Marquee Club Wardour Street. 1982

My one and only visit to the legendary Marquee Club was in March 1982 to see Magnum.

I have heard the Marquee club described as being the most important venue in the history of European pop music, simply because it existed to give room for the development of bands and artists right where the action was in the heart of London. From when it first opened in 1958 it became a vital hub for musicians in mainstream and progressive rock, the rhythm and blues scene as well as the punk and new wave movement.

The venue in Wardour Street, whilst in itself fairly plain, carried an aura, as well it should, with the vast list of legendary artists that have performed there, many of which might never have 'made it' had it not been for the opportunities of exposure that this iconic venue provided.

Magnum can hardly be listed alongside 'Marquee legends' such as the Stones, Hendrix, Bowie, Pink Floyd and Led Zeppelin, yet they have been a solid rock outfit that are still releasing quality albums and touring in the 2020s. They are what I call a 'Tolkienesque' band as many of their songs have a fantasy element – legends and fireside tales, kings and castles, knights and battles etc.

When I saw them in 1982, they had just released *'Chase the Dragon'*, a great album which they promoted in this show. It was a hot and sweaty all-in gig - but what else could you expect at the Marquee? [32]

---

[32] **The Marquee moved from Wardour St to Charing Cross in 1988 but sadly closed in 1996. Attempts to revive the club in the 2,000s never really took off.**

Chapter 21 – Theatrical Rock n Roll
Meat Loaf
Wembley Arena 1982

You know you're doing OK when your debut album immediately hits the charts on release and then stays there for... (wait for it) - NINE YEARS!

There's no question *'Bat out of Hell'* is one of the greatest rock albums of all time. Meat Loaf co-wrote the album with the brilliant Jim Steinman,[33] who also composed all the music. There weren't many people I knew who didn't at least know of the album and most it seemed, had a copy. So, when a tour was announced I was keen to check out the man behind the record.

The best way I can describe Meat Loaf live is rock theatre at its very best. It was a hugely entertaining show starting with the actual song *'Bat out of Hell'* complete with extended instrumental / guitar intro.

Meat Loaf tends to act out all his songs in a dramatic fashion – the ultimate example being the 3-part epic *'Paradise by the Dashboard Light'*, where a couple make out, fall out and walk out, all in one song. The 'argument' which happens in the middle of the song was extended, powerful and compelling – it appeared to be somewhat improvised, but was probably very well-rehearsed – either way, it would give any theatre drama a run for its money!

---

[33] **Also responsible for Bonnie Tyler's 'Total Eclipse of the Heart'**

The only downer was Meat Loaf's voice – he seemed to struggle with both range and quality. It was fortunate the band/backing singers were strong enough to cover up for his lack. Still, great music and fabulous theatrics; I suppose an appropriate conclusion would have to be *'Two out of three ain't bad.'*

WEMBLEY ARENA

I.T.B. Kennedy Street and Andrew Miller present

MEATLOAF

Monday, April 26th, 1982 at 8.00 p.m.

UPPER TIER SOUTH

£8.50

TO BE RETAINED   See conditions on back

APRIL **26** 1982

ENTER AT SOUTH DOOR ENTRANCE

60 ROW

C SEAT

109

Chapter 22 – Inflatable Juke Boxes
Foreigner
Wembley Arena 1982

Another journey to Wembley Arena, this time to see 'Foreigner', a Brit/ US rock band who were touring with the release of their album '4', a strong album that I had become familiar with. They had hit the charts with the ballad *'Waiting for a Girl Like You'*, which did no harm for ticket sales I'm sure, but in essence they were a solid rock band. One reason I was keen to go was to hear vocalist Lou Gramm, whose voice was powerfully emotive on record - and he didn't disappoint in the flesh. The transition to a live arena meant you not only heard but felt his voice. Truly worthy of an arena show.

It was a great night of which I particularly remember the following:

- A giant inflatable juke box appearing on stage during the song 'Juke Box Hero'.
- A brilliant sax solo during the track 'Urgent'.
- Great singalong time particularly to 'Cold as Ice' and encore, 'Hot Blooded'.

Foreigner won over the audience with a very good performance. Yet the best was still to come for them. Three years later the band returned to Wembley Arena. This was on the back of the mega hit, *I Wanna Know What Love Is.*' Result: They sold out eleven consecutive nights!

Chapter 23 - Supper's Ready
Genesis
Hammersmith Odeon 1982

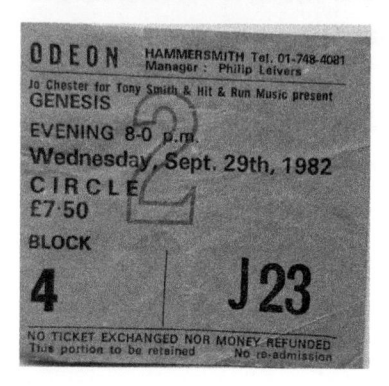

```
ODEON   HAMMERSMITH Tel. 01-748-4081
         Manager : Philip Leivers
Jo Chester for Tony Smith & Hit & Run Music present
GENESIS
EVENING 8-0 p.m.
Wednesday, Sept. 29th, 1982
CIRCLE
£7·50
BLOCK
4                    J 23
NO TICKET EXCHANGED NOR MONEY REFUNDED
This portion to be retained    No re-admission
```

For two years in my late teens, I had a job in the summer holidays working on a farm. For most of the time I was working on a potato machine and my job title was 'bagger'. It worked like this: the machine brought potatoes (mostly Crowns) up from the ground onto a conveyor belt, at the end of which were 2 bags located on scales. The potatoes would fill up the first bag and when it reached the correct weight, a lever was activated which flipped over to the second bag. The job of each of the two baggers was to lift off the full bag, tie it, stack it on a palette and put on a fresh bag <u>before</u> the scales flipped back again. Now most of the time this was OK, but on occasions, especially near the centre of the field, the Crowns were not only more numerous but tended to be the size of boulders. They would come thundering down the belt, filling up the bags in double quick time. Inevitably there were times when you just couldn't cope and it would end with the potatoes pouring off the end of the conveyor belt onto the floor and both baggers on the floor in fits of laughter buried under a pile of spuds.

Now I anticipate you may be wondering what on earth this has to do with Genesis. Well simply, that my fellow bagger was a big Genesis fan, and at this point I was just discovering the band, so all our lunch times and breaks would be spent either quoting Monty Python skits or talking Genesis.

I learnt so much band history from our conversations – from the early albums with Peter Gabriel as vocalist, to drummer Phil Collins becoming main singer, the departure of guitarist Steve Hackett leaving the iconic trio of Collins, Banks and Rutherford. We would discuss lyrics, album covers and imagery. We would also explore the meaning behind what we both agreed was our favourite Genesis song, the epic 'Supper's Ready'.

This is a twenty-three minute track off their 1972 album 'Foxtrot' split into seven sections concluding with a powerful apocalyptic themed ending. It is nothing short of a musical adventure, and has become (quite rightly) widely recognised as a cornerstone song for the prog rock genre.

Fast forward now four years or so and I'm back at the Hammy Odeon to see Genesis for the second time [c/f chapter 10].

This time it is very appropriate that my fellow gig goer was my old spud bagging mate, who had come down from Lincolnshire. Our friendship had continued post potatoes, and it was already a special evening, just going to see Genesis together. But we had no idea what surprises lay in store..

First though, I mentioned in Chapter 10 that I had been to see this band on four tours. So below are a few things that occurred each time I saw them, and why I kept coming back for more!

- The sound – always crystal clear and beautifully balanced. In all the shows I've seen Genesis play, the sound could never be faulted.

- The light show – Genesis always went for a spectacular lighting display as part of their show and combined it with a range of special effects.
- The drum duets - Due to Phil Collins being lead vocalist, Chester Thompson was the permanent drummer for the live shows. However, four or five times during a gig, Phil would take his place at a second kit where he would drum alongside Chester.

This for me was the highlight of any Genesis gig. I loved to see Collins play but seeing two world class drummers play together was something else! [34]

- The *'In the Cage'* medley' - this was included in every gig I went to. A brilliant medley starting with *'In the Cage'* (from *'The Lamb lies down on Broadway'*) and concluding with the amazing *Afterglow* (from *'Wind and Wuthering'*). In between was an instrumental medley which started with *'Cinema Show'* and then had another couple of songs which changed each tour (which was always a discussion point before and after).

- The Collins factor – Phil grew nicely into the role as frontman following Gabriel's departure. He was a born entertainer, interacting with the crowd and bringing a comedic aspect to the shows. Above all, his voice was fantastic.

All these aspects were present on this particular evening, but one thing neither of us anticipated or expected was when Collins announced after about half an hour that the next song was an older one called *'Supper's Ready'*. And lo and behold they played the whole song in its entirety. It felt like a gift for us and I think we both had a few tears in our eyes.

They never played the song in full again on any other tour. That's why of the four times I have seen Genesis, this gig topped the pile.

---

[34] **In the later tours the duet turned into a drum battle, with the two drummers trying to outdo one another. It started on stools (!) before moving onto the drum kit. [See Appendix A:9]**

It goes without saying that Genesis have been an important band in my life. In 2022, when they did a final tour as a farewell to fans, I would have liked to have gone but actually I am pleased I didn't. From footage I've since seen, it is more than sad to see Phil Collins unable to drum, barely able to walk or stand, and (although I hate to say it) struggling to sing (by comparison).

It would be an injustice if that had turned out to be my overriding memory of what has been one of the true great rock bands of all time. No, I'll stick with the wonderful drum duets, the medleys and the enduring memory of 'Supper's Ready' at Hammersmith 1982.

Chapter 24
Down Under
1983

Following the completion of my 3 years at Kingston, I decided to take a year out and embarked on an overseas 'world trip'.

I travelled with an old school mate, who gave up a dead-end job at the Post Office and we both obtained a one-year working visa for Australia. On arrival we managed to get jobs which looking back now, were really well paid and we were able to rent a flat in an Eastern suburb of Sydney, called Bronte, which was the 'next-door' bay/ beach to Bondi.

It was a life changing trip for both of us. For me, for example, I met and began a relationship with a kiwi girl called Kirsten, who eventually became my wife in 1988.

1983 was such a good time to be in Sydney. The city was vibrant and alive as indeed was the music industry. It seemed the world was waking up to what was happening down under and the music scene in particular was coming under the spotlight.

This was helped by:

The release of 'Men at Work's' brilliant song *'Down Under'* which was massive, first in Aussie and then across the world helping to add Vegemite sandwiches to global culinary menus.

David Bowie had just released his album *'Let's Dance'*, with videos for both the title track and *'China Girl'* singles being shot in Sydney, in what was a deliberate attempt to promote the city. It turned out he bought a waterfront apartment in the city in 1983 and owned it for ten years.

It was noticeable that more major artists seemed to be adding Australian cities to their touring itinerary.

Also, the era of MTV and the music video was at its peak; there was no shortage of music shows on Aussie TV playing all the new releases. We would often return from a night out and watch them into the early hours.

The power of music to awaken memories of past times is an amazing phenomenon. You can hear a song on the radio or see an old music video that maybe you haven't heard for years and suddenly it's like you're taken back in a time machine to a period in your life or an event, a day or even a moment.

For me, Michael Jackson's *'Beat it,'* U2's *'New Year's Day'*, Prince's *'Little Red Corvette'*, Elton John's *'I guess that's why they call it the Blues'* and *'Buffalo Gals'* by Malcolm McLaren are a few of the songs that when I hear them today, take me right back to that year in Sydney, and evoke nothing but great memories.

In addition to all this, I was fortunate to go to three memorable gigs.

1. Dire Straits at the Hordern Pavilion.

My travelling buddy and I had each bought a *Sony walkman for* our trip and spent three months visiting various countries en-route to Australia. That had given us plenty of listening time at airports and on flights. One band we had both come to love was Dire Straits who had at this time released *'Love over Gold'*. We had no idea that they would be playing in Sydney, a couple of months after our arrival.

DS at this time, were (in my opinion) at their peak, both in song writing and performing live. They played a perfect setlist (again, in my opinion) at this show, and it was a memorable night. I remember feeling full of joy coming out at the end.

This has got to be in my top ten best gigs of all time.

2. INXS *at 'Selina's' Coogee Bay Hotel*

Some bands you seem to develop a strange kind of connection with and INXS were one of those bands for Kirsten and I. For starters, this was the first gig we went to together. But more than that, it seemed we almost travelled their journey with them [c/f Chapter 32]. And it started here at a small music venue called 'Selinas', which was located within the Coogee Bay Hotel.[35] Despite being quite compact, it was starting to get a reputation as one of the top venues in Sydney for up-and-coming bands.

INXS were one of those bands. This five-piece Aussie outfit were formed in Sydney by the Farriss Brothers in the late 70s and had made a name locally playing the pub circuits of the city. Now having just made the Australian charts with a song called *'Don't Change'*, hype was building and they were touring wider afield to raise profile nationally. But this was a gig back on home turf.

As far as I can remember there were no tickets for this gig. I'm not too sure why - it may have been a last minute addition to the tour, but we just paid on the door.

Right from the word 'go' you could tell there was something special about this band. They had a unique sound and an outstanding charismatic singer in the form of Michael Hutchence, who was captivating to watch.

We came away from a great show convinced INXS would go far - and we were right!

---

[35] **Coogee Bay was our neighbouring beach/ bay on the other side of us to Bondi.**

3.10CC *at* 'Selina's' Coogee Bay Hotel

A rare and exciting gig experience is to see a big band play a small venue. Right here in Sydney an unexpected opportunity arose with British band 10CC.

It was in the early 70s when a talented quartet of musicians and songwriters combined their creativity and formed the band 10CC, releasing a number of great songs, three of which made No 1 in the UK along with other near misses. They were in a sense progressive pop, slightly out of the box, but not too much so as to alienate the mainstream audience. Such was their success they played to a 120,000 crowd at Knebworth in 1976.

Godley and Creme then split from the band in the late 70s leaving remaining members, Graham Gouldman and Eric Stewart to recruit replacements and continue. This is who we saw live that night.

I'm not sure quite how or why this gig came about – it may have been a warm up show for an upcoming UK tour which was due the following month, but why Sydney and why 'Selina's', I don't know! I do know tickets sold out quickly and we managed to get a couple before they did.

One of the lasting memories of this gig was that the band entered and exited the stage via a metal catwalk structure suspended above the heads of the audience. It was really cool.

As for the actual gig – wow – effectively a greatest hits set starting with *Rubber Bullets* and ending with their biggest song, a hit worldwide: *I'm Not in Love*.

Finally, we were sent off into the night with the amazing guitar solos within the encore song *'Feel the Benefit'*.

This is one of those gigs where my appreciation has grown over the years. I have only ever seen 10CC this once, and I consider myself fortunate that I was able to be part of this intimate gig.

```
SELINAS
COOGEE BAY HOTEL
COOGEE

10CC

CLOSED BAR DURING 10CC
FRI 9TH SEPT '83 FROM 7PM
```

UNRESERVED		ADULT
SEP GA	GA-407	10.60

Chapter 25
A New Year's Eve Surprise
Wembley Arena 1983

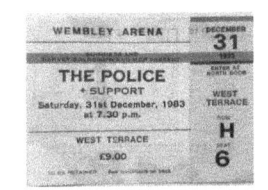

Back from my global travels, I was keen to catch up with some old friends who I hadn't seen for eighteen months, so a group of us arranged to meet in London and do the Trafalgar Square New Year's Eve thing (which was the thing before the London eye fireworks thing today).

So, we met in the West End and had a couple of drinks, and discussions ensued as to what we should do before Trafalgar Square. Included in the suggestions were a theatre show or a gig. Everyone there had been a fellow gig-goer at one time or another, so it seemed the ideal choice but none of us had any idea of who was playing in London. Don't forget this was all pre-mobiles. Whereas today, instant access to information is one tap away, back in the early 80s there was no such technology.

My memory is a bit hazy as to what happened next. I think we went to some kind of ticket booth who sold tickets to various events, and I think it was here we discovered the Police were playing a run of gigs at Wembley Arena, but that it was all sold out.

We decided on the spur of the moment to get the tube out to Wembley on the off chance there were some tickets available. If not, we figured we could hit a local pub and then return to the West End.

An hour later and we were at the Arena where the crowds and atmosphere had started to build. No luck at the box office though. We found out tonight's gig was the last night of a Wembley run, and all shows had been sold out for weeks.

We then did something I had never done before nor done since. We approached some ticket touts. They were offering tickets at twice face value. We tried to negotiate but couldn't get them to shift. So, we strategically walked away and went for a couple more drinks. Then, about 8pm, we figured the support band must have started so we returned to the same tout and this time had more success. After negotiation we were able to get a ticket each together and paid £3 over the face value price. We were in. By the time we entered the arena, the support band, 'The Animals' were near the end of their set but we did catch *House of the Rising Sun*.

And then the Police!

I don't know what it was about tonight, but I had probably one of the most fun nights of any gig. Whether it was the New Year's Eve factor or the fact that we'd had a few drinks or whether the fact that I had started the day with no idea I was even going to a gig and therefore had no expectation, I don't know. But we all had a real party.

It didn't seem to matter what song the band threw at us - *'Message in a Bottle'*, *'Walking on the*

Moon', 'So Lonely' or 'Don't Stand so Close', we responded to Sting's impromptu singalongs with our own 'YEH oh oh oh's' at every twist and turn. It hit the spot right where we were at, and I can remember not wanting it to end. A fantastic night! This was the only time I have engaged the services of a tout, and I'm so pleased I did. I wouldn't have missed this for the world. By the way, we just made Trafalgar Square for midnight with minutes to spare. This was a night when the planets aligned!

Tout Confessions

"Any Spares?"

For most of my gig-going life, one feature that was guaranteed at every event was the ticket touts. As soon as you arrived at the tube/ bus/ train station close to the venue, there they were with their familiar cry: *"Anyone need a ticket? I'll buy any spares!!"*.

A ticket tout is someone who buys bulk tickets at face value and then sells them on at a profit, sometimes a hefty one. The question is though – is this ripping fans off or providing a genuine service?

Laws have been brought in to make touting illegal but this was specifically directed at football matches, with the motivation of the legislation being to avoid rival fans being enclosed together in the same sections. But it is not illegal as such to resell a ticket to a concert or gig.

Of course, along with the move to online ticket purchases, the number of touts outside venues has declined and, in some cases, disappeared, as they have reverted to online web sites. This has only led to increased activity with professional touts 'harvesting' tickets, restricting supply to genuine fans.

Adele recently tried to deny resellers any access to her sold out tour, but despite her best efforts, tickets with a face value of £100 were sold on resale sites like *'Viagogo'* for over £700

In December 2022 however, in what could be a landmark

case, 2 ticket touts who operated on a massive scale were ordered to pay back £6,167,522.02 at a hearing at Leeds Crown Court. How that will impact the future, only time will tell.

Over the years I have had several conversations with people about touts. Some of those people I've had discussions with have voiced strong opinions. I've even heard the word 'scum' associated with those involved.

Yet honestly, I never have seen things that way. Whilst I'm opposed to the vast mafia scale online industry, I've never had a problem with touts outside venues selling tickets because of course there was always a risk for them too. I've known people buy tickets from touts at well under ticket value, due to a gig proving to be not as popular as first thought, leaving a surplus. So, it's not one way traffic. And if the prices are offered at inflated rates– well, you don't have to pay them, do you? If you choose to, then it's obviously worth it to you.

To me the result is there is an opportunity to see a gig you otherwise couldn't see…like (for me) the Police gig on New Year's eve. Without touts, I would never have had that experience and created that amazing memory.

So just for those small-scale touts who were/are trying to earn a living, I know all the abuse you've put up with, so from me, just a quiet and belated *Thank you* for that evening in 1983 and you know what? Now it's not there, I have come to realise that hearing the dulcet tones of 'Any Spares?' on venue arrival has been all part of the gig going experience. You know you'd arrived!

Would it be terribly wrong to confess that 'I miss it?'

Chapter 26 - Turning Point
Simple Minds
Hammersmith Odeon 1984

This gig was Kirsten's doing. Simple Minds were one of her favourite bands who she had followed in New Zealand. Sadly, at that time, the opportunities to see a band like that in NZ were rare with only the biggest acts being able to meet the costs of bringing their show on tour. What a contrast to London, with amazing opportunities for live music by classic artists and emerging talent every night of the week.

Simple Minds were labelled as part of the 'new romantic' or 'art pop' genre, and it was outside my comfort zone. I set a course to familiarise myself with some of the back catalogue of the band. Eventually I connected to the album *'New Gold Dream'* which had some good tracks, including the groovy *'Promised you a Miracle.'*

My surprise at the gig was how much more 'rockier' Simple Minds were. Tracks off the new album *'Sparkle in the Rain'* such as *'Waterfront'* and *'Speed your Love to me'* had a pumping rock bass beat and provided bold variations on both sound and feel.

In hindsight I now see this was a real 'turning point' time for the band, in transitioning to the mainstream. Following this tour and album came the anthemic *'Don't You Forget about Me'* and No. 1 single *'Belfast Child'*. Of course, singer Jim Kerr's marriage to

The Pretenders, Chrissie Hynde, did no harm for band publicity[36]. The marriage lasted six years. Fortunately, the band have had more success and are still together some forty years later, selling out arenas.

---

[36] **The wedding took place May 5th 1984, one week before our gig.**

Chapter 27 – Time Passages
Al Stewart
Royal Albert Hall 1984

*"I felt the beat of my mind go drifting into Time Passages.
Years go falling in the fading light.
Time Passages. Buy me a ticket on the last train home tonight.
Hear the echoes and feel yourself starting to turn.
Don't know why you should feel that there's something to learn.
It's just a game that you play…"*

My first visit to what has become one of my favourite venues over the years: the magnificent Royal Albert Hall.

This distinctive round building with its iconic dome is tucked away overlooking Kensington Gardens. It was opened by Queen Victoria in 1871 and today seats just over 5,000 people in the main auditorium hosting a vast variety of different events and concerts, probably most famously, the Proms.

So, what is it about the RAH that is so special for gigs?

- The seating design is such that you never feel too far from the stage. That's because the focus is on height rather than length/ breadth.
- The sound has always been impressive when I've been there, although the dome apparently caused distortion issues until acoustic 'mushrooms' were installed in the late 1960s. More recently, a new state of the art sound system was introduced comprising of 465 permanently installed

individual speakers, meaning wherever you sit, you get the same quality sound.

Mostly however, unlike anywhere else, there is a powerful sense of history. Once you pass through the ticket check and leave the entrance foyer, you arrive at a circular corridor that extends right round the building. Hung on the walls are framed photos of past performances and events. It is like walking through a passage of time and I felt a sense of awe that such important and varied gatherings have happened "right here". From meetings by the Suffragettes to exhibition boxing bouts by Muhammad Ali, as well as key speeches by Winston Churchill and Albert Einstein. But as my eyes rested on each exhibit in turn, there grew a dawning awareness that the fabric of the building has absorbed sounds from the cream of worldwide performers over the decades: Shirley Bassey, Eric Clapton, Adele, The Beatles, Jimi Hendrix, Oasis, Frank Sinatra, The Beach Boys, Michael Jackson...the list goes on.

Tonight, it was the turn of folk-rock singer and guitarist, Al Stewart to grace the famous stage. Al is a stalwart of popular music. He played at the first ever Glastonbury, shared lodgings with Paul Simon, and was friends with Yoko Ono before she knew John Lennon.

I had discovered Al's music over the last couple of years and loved the way he weaves historical events and characters into his songs and tells their

```
ROYAL ALBERT HALL
GENERAL MANAGER: D. CAMERON McNICOL
THE FACE OF THIS DOCUMENT HAS A COLOURED BACKGROUND
         WEDNESDAY 30TH. MAY 1984
         AT 1930.DOORS OPEN AT 1845

                PLP PRESENTS
         AN EVENING WITH AL STEWART
                PLUS GUESTS.
ADMIT TO:-
                  STALLS 'J'
                ENTER BY DOOR 4
                PRICE (INC. VAT)   ROW    SEAT

475 0889 N        £7.50            7      674

THE BACK OF THIS DOCUMENT CONTAINS AN ARTIFICIAL WATERMARK
TO BE RETAINED                  See Reverse
```

story with often a modern-day twist. He frequently performs acoustic solo gigs but this show was with a full band, a highlight being the showcase of his most famous song – the classic *'Year of the Cat'* complete with extended guitar and sax solo.

It was also significant that on the set list was another favourite *'Time Passages'* which seemed an appropriate salute to the sense of history of this wonderful concert hall.

This was a different sort of gig, and a real joy to sit and enjoy great musicianship and skilful storytelling, which occurred in his verbal introduction to songs as well as the songs themselves).

This sat so nicely alongside the fact the venue tells its own story, and that by attending a show, in a small way you become part of the story.

"Time Passages. There's something back here that you left behind. Oh time passages. Buy me a ticket on the last train home tonight" [37]

---

[37] **The lyrics at the beginning and end of his chapter are from Al Stewart's 'Time Passages', the title track off his eighth studio album released in 1978.**

Chapter 28 – Still Standing
Elton John
NEC Birmingham 1984

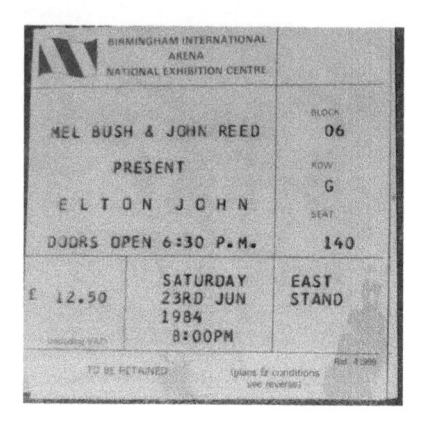

After a tough few years, Elton's popularity was back on track following the success of his *'Too Low for Zero'* album, from which emerged the huge hit single *'I'm Still Standing'*.

This gig was part of the *'Breaking Hearts'* tour introducing *'Sad Songs (say so much)'* into the set alongside the already large catalogue of hits – *'Tiny Dancer'*, *'Rocket Man'*, *'Candle in the Wind,'* *'Your Song'* and encores *'Goodbye Yellow Brick Road'* and *'Crocodile Rock'*.

Elton was out to prove he was still 'King of the Camp'. He hit the stage in a nice up-market cowboy outfit, complete with white hat, boots, metallic gold jacket, and of course, large white rimmed glasses. Suits you Sir! He wisely paced himself sandwiching his quieter songs at the piano with his up-tempo rockers, where he became energetically stage bound, parading and jumping around.

This was a thoroughly enjoyable concert, although the sound wasn't great. That seemed to be a combination of his voice and the NEC's sound system. However, there was a clear statement of intention: Elton was back with a bang, and we were reminded of the vast catalogue of great songs in his repertoire, leaving us in no doubt that he would be here to stay.

Chapter 29 – The End of the Road?
Status Quo
Milton Keynes Bowl 1984

When a band announces it's the end of the road and advertise a final gig – that means they are going to stop playing, making records and touring – right?

I confess, I've been a bit confused for the last forty years because in 1984, Status Quo announced they were splitting up after twenty two years together and their final show <u>ever</u> would be at the Milton Keynes Bowl on 21st July 1984.

Quo were a strange band to me. I didn't love them, but I liked them a lot. I found them a bit like a Chinese takeaway. You looked forward to it immensely, and knew what you were going to get. When it arrived and was served up, the first tastes were delicious. However, you rapidly seemed to get full and got to the point when you couldn't handle another mouthful. But then before you know it, you're up for some more.

I had seen Status Quo three times to date – Hammersmith Odeon 1979, Wembley 1981 and as headliners in the third Monsters of Rock festival at Donington in 1982. There is no doubt I enjoyed them all, but after each one I left with a *'that's enough of that – I'm done with Quo now!'* mindset, only to be back next time. I mentioned just now that whenever you went to a Quo gig you always knew what you were in for. For example, in all three gigs above, the set lists varied little. They started with the same three songs beginning with *'Caroline'* and finished with the same encores *'Down Down'* and *'Bye Bye Johnny'*, and inbetween were ninety minutes of non-stop guitar led rock hits, most at the same tempo and using the same three chords.

When this gig was announced I remember thinking should I go? Shouldn't I go? I'd seen it all before but as it's the last Hurrah I think I could just about handle one more Chinese meal for old times' sake.

And so off to the Milton Keynes Bowl I go, to bid farewell to Quo for the final time.

The line-up at this one-day festival was an interesting mix. American Country rock band 'Jason and the Scorchers' were up first. I thought they did OK, but most of the crowd didn't seem to agree and they got bombarded with beer bottles and other containers not just filled with beer!

Next were Scottish band Nazareth, who I knew through a string of hits in the mid-late 70s the best-known being *'Love Hurts'*. Gravelly voiced singer Dan McCaffety was in great form and they went down well.

Gary Glitter must have been nervous having seen the reaction of the crowd to Jason & the Scorchers. But with an OTT performance of sheer genius, combining outrageous antics, singalong classics and full glitter outfits, he went down a storm. (This was the first-time seeing GG live and there would several more to come. – c/f Chapter 40)

This was also the first time (again of several more to come) that I saw what was the main support band, Marillion – a relatively new prog rock band in the mould of early Peter Gabriel era Genesis. I'd had a listen to some of their songs to get a taste prior to this gig, and what I'd heard was intriguing. It didn't take me long to realise the band had a big following and the fans, all crammed at the front, could recite every word of every tongue-twisting lyric, leaving me wishing I'd known more to be able to join in. The singer called Fish was captivating. With his large frame, he commanded the stage like a Shakespearian actor, bearing a face paint 'mask' and acting out every song. I absolutely loved every minute of this set and I knew that this band would be a part of my future.

And finally – The Headliners!

The Quo army were out in full force for this 'last ever gig'! Around 40,000 of us were treated to two hours of non-stop guitar led rock, full of hit songs played at the same tempo and using the same three chords. They started the set with *'Caroline'* and finished with encores *'Down Down'* and *'Bye Bye Johnny'*... and let's face it, we'd all have been disappointed if it had been anything else.

A firework finale of some note finished the evening and it's Goodbye, Farewell and Thank you Status Quo!

Except the following year 1985 they kicked off the 'Live Aid' event at Wembley Stadium, and the year after that in 1986, they were back on the road for an extensive European tour.

'End of the Road' my A**E!

If I hadn't had such a good time, I may have been making enquiries as whether it's too late to get a refund!

Sadly 2016 really was the 'end of the road' for legendary guitarist and co-founder of Quo, Rick Parfitt who died on Christmas Eve that year.

Yet still, led on by only original member Francis Rossi, the band continue to perform, record and tour on what has turned out to be 'an endless road' rather than 'end of the road.' Of course, we can't rule out the possibility of another farewell gig. After all, I may be starting to get hungry again!

Quo – Again and again and again and again and again and again and again and..

Chapter 30 – Take Me Home (I Don't Remember)
Phil Collins
Royal Albert Hall 1985

Great to be back at the RAH and to see Phil Collins, although I confess, I don't remember too much about the gig. This may have been partially due to the fact that I didn't feel too good. I do recall a substantial backing band called 'The Hot Tub Club' which included Chester Thompson on drums and as per Genesis, there was some great double drumming. I remember *'In the Air tonight'* being a highlight and also the final song: *'Take me Home- I don't remember'* which seemed somewhat appropriate considering how I had been feeling. Don't get me wrong this was a top-quality gig - I just wasn't in the zone!

Chapter 31 – Finger Pickin' good
Dire Straits
Wembley Arena 1985

Two years ago, I saw Dire Straits in Sydney (c/f Chapter 24), and here I was again - this time on the other side of the globe in London. It was fitting my gig-going companions on this occasion were my old travelling buddy who had been with me at the Sydney gig, and our future wives (both kiwis).

This was one of a run of thirteen sold-out shows at Wembley Arena for Dire Straits and interestingly this show was the same week as Live Aid[38] at which they also performed. In my opinion, the band had passed their peak of song production, yet they were still at the top of their game when it came to live shows.

Mark Knopfler is one of the world's best guitarists ever. His 'finger-picking' style is unique and instantly recognisable. He has the ability to make his guitar talk. Watching (or listening to) him live on faster songs such as *'Sultans of Swing'* immediately explains why he doesn't use a pick – the speed of playing is simply too fast for a pick to be used (although if the evidence was not right before you, one may question whether it would be possible with fingers!!).

---

[38] **Our night was the Sunday and Live Aid was the following Saturday. On this day, Dire Straits performed their short set mid-late afternoon at the Stadium and then scarpered back across the road to perform a full concert at the Arena.**

The other thing I love about Dire Straits is the constant live re-working of the songs. 'Romeo and Juliet' is a great example. It is on the setlist of every tour, yet every time it's re-worked. With the inclusion of piano, sax, and other instruments working in with Knopfler's guitar work to create powerful and memorable music.

Tonight, we get both *'Sultans'* and *"Romeo'* plus *'Tunnel of Love '*and for the first time *'Brothers in Arms'*. Perhaps to be fair, not quite reaching the heights of the Sydney gig, but still truly wonderful!

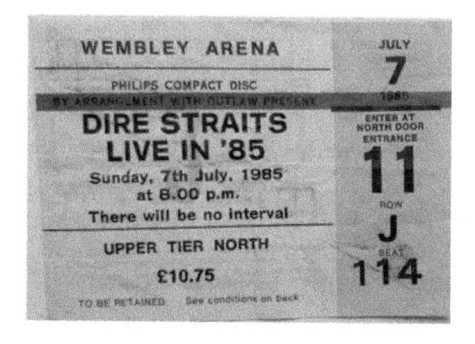

Live Aid Confessions

What book on Gig-going wouldn't include 'Live Aid'?

Well, this one! Because I have to confess, I wasn't there. Oh, I so dearly wish I had been because for my particular lifespan of gig-going, this has to be the pinnacle of all concerts. It was the day 'Music changed the World'. I think it's the musical equivalent to the assassination of JFK in the sense you remember what you were doing and where you were at the time. And I do!

July 13th 1985 - I was living in Norfolk at the time of this Bob Geldof organised Charity concert. I remember:

1. Watching the start on TV with Status Quo opening the Wembley show with the iconic *'Rockin' all over the World'*, which had in a sense become the event's theme song.
2. Driving to Lincolnshire to my parents listening on the radio, and arriving in time to see U2's set on TV.
3. Queen's unforgettable 20 min set widely perceived to be the greatest live performance ever.
4. The amazing moment when Philadelphia joined up with London for the simultaneous broadcast.
5. Phil Collins double appearance at Wembley and immediately jetting to Philadelphia and performing there.
6. The moving video to the Cars *'Drive'*, spurring the giving to a reported £125 Million.

Owning the DVD of this event serves to remind me of the amazing line up and the pioneering nature of the concert.

Chapter 32 – The Pheromone Machine
INXS
UEA Norwich 1986

Our journey with this band continued. After seeing them in a small venue in hometown Sydney (c/f Chapter 24) and then explode nationally in Australia, now they attempt to repeat the cycle in the UK. How special is it that included in their UK tour is a date just down the road in Norwich. The venue is perhaps on par with *Selina's* size wise and so this was deja-vu indeed.

It was another fantastic gig, and I remember leaving convinced they would grow to be massive in the UK. ... and of course, they did, but not only the UK, pretty much globally.

Undoubtedly, one of the reasons for the success of the band as well as their unique sound, is the charismatic nature of singer Michael Hutchence. A rich emotive voice and a great performer but he also had another aspect that was rare yet noticeable. He oozed sensuality. It's a hard thing to explain. It's not a physical, external attractiveness (in fact Hutchence had quite bad acne/skin complaint in his early days). Rather it is something that exudes from within. It was like his presence could change the atmosphere of a room. – he brought an edge, an excitement, almost a danger. I was reminded of this recently when I came across a clip from Jools Holland's 'Later' show back in 1994 where Hutchence performed a toned down version of 'Never Tear us apart' sitting on a piano (Still from this show below)

Hutchence – giving off the vibes

He was, in the words of Kirsten, *"a walking pheromone machine"* (said with a twinkle in her eye!). The only other performer I have seen that carried a similar sensual charisma, was Prince.

Sadly, Michael Hutchence's personal life did not mirror the success of the band. A series of high-profile relationships with singer Kylie Minogue, model Helena Christensen and TV presenter Paula Yates, caused media frenzy. With the latter, Hutchence had a daughter in 1996 called Tiger Lily. But then tragically the following year, Michael was found dead in a Sydney hotel room, having taken his own life whilst being under the influence of drugs. Paula spiralled into depression and three years later died of a heroin overdose at her home, leaving Tiger Lily an orphan.

It's hard to fathom this tragic story and we can never know what events transpired that led to the untimely loss of such precious lives. All we can do is to continue to enjoy the music and memories of a singer and a band that really mattered to us.

Chapter 33 – Simply the Best
Queen
Wembley Stadium 1986

Every now and again, I get asked what my best gig of all time is. Sometimes weaved in alongside this question is a comment like 'with you having seen so many top bands & concerts, it must be impossible to choose a favourite?'

But it actually isn't!

The answer without hesitation is always *"Queen Wembley 1986"*. It's a no brainer for me. Why? Freddie's last gig (for me), and also his best gig (for me), an unbelievable performance from Queen as a whole, the perfect setting of Wembley Stadium, the ideal support band line up, shared with my wife and great friends, all big Queen fans... need I go on?

The day unfolded as follows:

INXS – Again, how amazing that this band are selected to open the show – we couldn't have scripted it better. So, two months after seeing them perform in the relatively humble environment of a uni campus, here they are propelled to play on arguably the biggest stage of them all. Despite all that I'm sure it's never easy being first band on stage in a concert of this magnitude. Yet they did great, got a rousing reception and did their job. This was the last time we saw INXS, and it was fitting that it was on the big stage. There was one other show I would like to have been at, but sadly we were overseas. This was the band's return to Wembley Stadium in 1991. This time they were the headliners, and managed to sell out the 72,000 tickets. Fortunately, this gig was filmed and officially released under the title of *'Live Baby Live Wembley Stadium'*, for all to enjoy and remember.

THE ALARM – In fact our gig going friends' favourite band, who we had already seen several times in smaller venues, but here was a rare chance to see them on a big stage. Led by Mike Peters, I viewed this band as pioneers of anthemic rock alongside U2. It could be argued that a stadium setting is the right environment for this genre. And The Alarm worked hard to prove this point. Massive songs like *'Spirit of 76'* and *'Strength'* rung around the rafters of the stadium and they were perfect for the occasion.

STATUS QUO – Hang on, I thought these guys had done their last ever gig two years ago? Oh, that's right, they did... and here we go again. Yes, I was looking forward to seeing the Quo for one last (or one more) time. Yes, they were great and yes, *'Caroline'* was at the start and *'Bye Bye Johnny'* at the end... and so until the next time....??

QUEEN - All I can say is this was the perfect show. It is of course captured in full on DVD 'Queen Live at

Wembley' as a lasting memento. The fact that it has been recorded has done two things: for those who were there, it has helped preserve the memory, which always fades over time. For those who weren't there, it has provided an iconic benchmark for the live stadium gig.

From the legendary 'One Vision' opening, the band were on top form and Freddie gave the complete performance both vocally and as a front man. It's very hard to pick out highlights there were so many:

- 'Who wants to Live Forever' was magnificent with the purity and power of the vocals verberating around the stadium.
- The sight of the sea of raised clapping arms during 'Radio Ga Ga'
- Freddie's leading of the crowd in vocal gymnastics was brilliant.
- When the band launched into 'It's A Kind of Magic', four inflatable balloons appeared, each one the figure of a band member identical to the caricatures on the 'Magic' album. When inflated they are released into the air. Almost immediately two perish at the hands of a grabbing crowd. The third (I think it's John!) bounces around the crowd for a few seconds and then bursts. But the fourth hovers above the crowd and then slowly starts to rise up. It's Freddie! And up he goes, out of the stadium and onwards rising higher and higher up into the stratosphere encouraged on by the crowd,

until he fades out of sight. A fun (and in hindsight a poignant) moment.[39]

However, my over-riding memory was right at the end of the show, during the closing bars of *'We are the Champions'* when Freddie disappears off stage briefly, only to return with royal robe and crown, slowly walking to the front of the stage in true regal, processional style, lifting the crown to acknowledge the crowd, before taking the final bow.

That was the last time I saw Freddie, and that image is a fitting one to be seared in the memory.

---

[39] In 2014, Brian May posted on his website news that the inflatable Freddie had landed at Leigh on Sea in Essex and posted a photo of a family with it. One mystery solved! A second however is why it took 28 years to come to light?

Chapter 34 - Short-changed
Bob Dylan / Tom Petty
Wembley Arena 1986

Kirsten, who ironically was the big Dylan fan, caught a nasty flu bug, so with disappointment all around, I ended up at this gig alone. The ticket stated a side view, but it proved to be a good position overlooking the stage.

This was the third of four nights at Wembley for Dylan. The show was in two parts. The first half was a set by Tom Petty & The Heartbreakers. Then after an interval, Bob Dylan did his set with T.P. & the band fulfilling the role of his backing band.

Well, the first half was great. Tom Petty was outstanding, playing a tight, professional and energetic set. He seemed very relaxed, clearly enjoying the occasion. There were a few cover versions of songs along with a selection of the best of his own. Highlights for me were *'American Girl'* and *'Refugee'*. The class and experience shone clearly.

Then onto the second half.

I confess I wasn't the biggest Dylan fan, but because of Kirsten I had been introduced to quite a few of his songs, and had come to appreciate the lyrical genius of his song writing. Despite the sadness of Kirsten's absence, I was nevertheless appreciative for the opportunity to see a true legend live.

Now it's no secret that Dylan can be rather moody at times, and it seemed that by pure chance, tonight happened to be one of those times. He came on and played a fifty minute set with virtually no audience interaction, walked off at the end and didn't appear for an encore. It really was hugely disappointing. When the house lights came on there was clear disgruntlement from the crowd with jeers and a few boos – an appropriate response for what was a heartless and soulless performance. He did himself no favours among the crowd that night.

I don't know whether there were any formal repercussions but it's interesting that I discovered that the following night he played a twenty song set as opposed to fourteen on my night. The extra songs included four classics all of which I knew and really liked; '*The Times they are a Changin'*, '*Be my Baby Tonight'*, '*Knocking on Heavens Door'* and '*Don't Think Twice its Alright'*.

Although Tom Petty had already saved the day for me, I can't help thinking I'd been a bit short-changed!

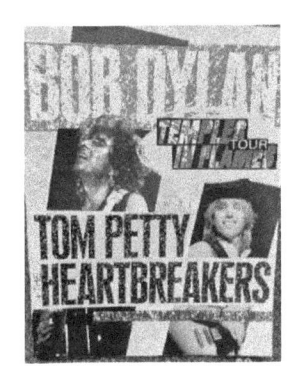

Set List Confessions

To know or not to know? – that is the question!

Any gig-going enthusiast will tell you that one of the main talking points both before and after a concert is '**what did they play?**' The traditional construction of a setlist would be a mixture of new songs (probably from an upcoming or recently released record) alongside the hits/ favourites. For some artists that have been going for (say) five to ten years, this can be predictable, simply because their output of material is just about right for a strong live set.

But predictability is not necessarily a bad thing. Over the years of gig-going, I have certainly learnt there's a 'formula' which involves playing the right songs at the right time, and if it's discovered and followed, the return for both artist and audience is immensely rewarding. I have seen bands try and break the mould with a new formula, probably to avoid being stereotypical. So, for example they may play all new material or play their best-known song early in the set, or even finishing the encore with a new song. My conclusion is that this rarely works. For a gig-goer, it can be frustrating and disappointing leaving a show not having heard the song(s) you really wanted to hear.

Of course, it really gets interesting when you have a band that have been going for years and have lots of albums under their belt and enough 'hits' to fill two setlists or more. The dilemma for these performers is *What on earth do we play? What do we leave out?* This then becomes an eager point of discussion for the gig-goer…which then brings into play the BIG Question at the start…

To know or not to know?

Most regular gig-goers will be aware of the website Setlist FM. [If not, I may have just ruined your life!] Basically, it is a wonderful resource and database for the gig history of any band/ artist. You can type in a name and instantly get not only a list of concerts and venues played, but complete setlists from any year. [That's how I discovered the extra songs Dylan played at Wembley in the last chapter]. But the other aspect is you can search the band you are going to see tomorrow night and find out their setlist from last night. The high majority of bands will keep the setlists for a tour the same with the odd variation maybe, but in essence, you can find out in advance what they will play.

To know or not to know? What is your opinion?

I confess over the years, I've done the whole spectrum. There are times I would have hated to know the setlist prior to the show, believing it would spoil the surprise and anticipation of the night. In fact, I have been to a gig where I've had to ask a fellow gig goer to stop announcing what song is coming up next. But there's also been times, where I've followed setlists of tours right up until my show and knowing what is being played has added to the excitement. I've even checked out a setlist to determine whether or not I buy a ticket! So, it seems that 'to know or not to know' is too simplistic a question as there are differing factors that may direct my actions. It seems the type of gig or the band itself, or the age factor or just how I'm feeling right now, are all influencers.

So, the real question perhaps is - *Why isn't anything simple?*

Chapter 35 – Dancing in Stilettoes
Marillion
Hammersmith Odeon 1986 and Wembley Arena 1987

It was a freezing cold evening as Kirsten & I made our way to Wembley Arena, which was around a thirty minute walk from where we'd parked. She was wearing heels and we were debating if the footwear was an inappropriate choice with the fact that it was a bit icy underfoot. Almost immediately, a line from Marillion's best known song *'Kayleigh'* came to her mind: *'Dancing in Stilettoes in the snow'*, and suddenly it seemed to be very appropriate.

Since my introduction to Marillion at the Milton Keynes Bowl in 1984 (c/f Chapter 29), both K & I had invested time getting to know this band. We had watched them grow in popularity and following. We saw them play at the Hammersmith Odeon in 1986 introducing what is probably one of the best concept albums ever written: *'Misplaced Childhood'*, and playing it in its entirety. A year later and they are now playing a sold-out show at Wembley Arena, in what many would view as a 'We've made it' gig.

This time they were promoting what is an equally brilliant record: *'Clutching at Straws'*.

Fish, (now without painted face) and the band were ready for this, taking to the stage after a lengthy intro of the rousing classical piece *'The Thieving Magpie'* by Rossini and launched straight into a superb opener, *'Slainte Mhath'* off *'Clutching at Straws'*. We had seats on the flat arena floor, about a third of the way back – great seats except that naturally, everyone stood at the start and Kirsten despite wearing heels, couldn't see due to several towering Marillion fans in the row in front. So, at the start of the gig, she climbed on her chair, which made her fractionally taller than me, and in that position, we enjoyed the whole gig, together with a great view.

It was a magnificent night, concluding with a *'Kaleigh'/ 'Lavender'/ 'Heart of Lothian'* medley. It felt like we were celebrating a milestone for the band. Sadly, factions saw Fish leave after this tour, so in hindsight it felt like 'moment in time' mountain top concert, that was wonderful to be a part of.

Fish - Leads the Wembley Crowd home

Chapter 36 – An Entertainment Masterpiece
Michael Jackson
Wembley Stadium 1988

The sense of anticipation was like nothing I had experienced before. We had been in our seats located to the side of the stadium for several hours now.
- We had seen the slow crowd build up.
- We had watched Kim Wilde as support act and we had sung along to 'Kids in America'.
- We had endured numerous 'Mexican waves' (c/f Page 218)
- We had watched the arrival of the Prince and Princess of Wales take their seats on the opposite side of the stadium to us, and any moment now we would see what we had come to see.

I could feel the excitement not only within myself but within the mass of souls within the stadium. It is hard to describe and without wanting to seem over dramatic, it seemed to crackle like spiritual electricity.

Suddenly, the stage darkens and brooding music crescendos amidst swirling dry ice. The crowd noise is phenomenal. A bank of lights running at the back of the stage slowly get brighter until it is almost blinding. Then they start to fade away and what before was an empty stage now has Michael Jackson centre stage with two male dancers either side of him – all five figures like statues. And then the band blasts into *'You Wanna be Startin' Something'*.

An incredible start to what really turned out to be a concert that is hard to rival. I recall an article by John Peel after the event who described it as *'a show I do not expect to see equaled in my lifetime.'*. And the key to me here, is the word 'show'. Because this wasn't just a series of songs but more dramatized scenes complete with costume changes, in each one, Jackson leading his fantastic team of dancers, who played their part in the action. Sometimes they danced in contrast to Michael, at other times in complete sync, performing identical routines to the iconic videos with such authority - the dancing undead in *'Thriller'*, the street gang battle of *'Beat it'* and the seedy underworld of *'Smooth Criminal.'*

As amazing as these choreographed masterpieces were, the moments when Jackson was alone on stage were equally mesmerising; particularly *'Bad'* with heavy rock guitar mayhem and *'Billie Jean'* with an extended dance sequence of body popping, moonwalking, kicking, twirling, crotch grabbing and general movement of limbs at such speed at times, that you wouldn't have thought humanly possible.

Add to all this a Jackson 5 medley, a duet with Sheryl Crow (*'I Just Can't Stop Loving You'*), a joyful *'Rock with You'*, and several magic moments – literally. At one point a tent descends over Jackson, rising a few seconds later with him having disappeared. Then an explosion of light and he's on the other side of the stage on a platform launching into a new song.

It was impossible not to be caught up in the spectacle and with occasional glances through the binoculars at the Royal couple, they too appeared to be well into it. (Well half of them anyway!). There was some pre-gig media discussion as to whether MJ would perform *'Dirty Diana'* and if he did whether it may be offensive to the Prince and Princess of Wales? Well, he did, and a further glance through the binoculars revealed Diana up and grooving!

The show lasted just over two hours – there was a slight break half way through for Jackson while the band played a solo section, but the energy expended by him never really dipped through the whole show. It was an extraordinary performance, one could even say dangerous - ahh, now <u>that</u> would make a great title for a future album.

Chapter 37 – Musical Genius
Prince
Wembley Arena 1988 and NEC Birmingham 1990

Just this last week, I was driving in the car with Kirsten and a Prince song came on the radio, That's not unusual. Neither was my comment, *"Ah, I'm so pleased we got to see Prince"*. I don't know how many times I've said those words, and even more times thought them.

There is no artist quite like Prince. He created so much music, over so long, in so many different styles, always on the edge and always experimenting with new sounds. He is the most overall talented pop/rock star that I have ever seen, if not ever known. I have to use the word 'genius' because of all the aspects and areas that make up a performing musician, Prince seemed to have a completeness in them all.

HIS VOCALS – He had not only an amazing range of notes (from bottom to top registers) but an amazing range of 'voices'. What I mean is his style changed from song to song more than anyone else I know. From bluesy to gospel, rock to funk, jazz to dance, he could sound innocent, seductive, celebratory, forlorn, sexy, dreamy and mysterious, all on one album!

HIS SONGWRITING – There was no style of pop composition that Prince couldn't master - from songs of sophisticated complexity to those of two chord simplicity. He knew the 'tools' of song writing and how to maximise potential in key structure, chord progression and the use of intros outros and bridges. He knew how to make an infectious melody, that would stick in the mind of a listener. No proof is necessary on this, other than to recognise the legacy of not only his own vast catalogue of classic hits, but the numerous artists who have found success in recording his songs. The best known probably being *'Kiss'* by Tom Jones, *'Manic Monday'* by the Bangles, and *'Nothing Compares to You'* by Sinead O'Connor.

HIS LYRICS – Covered everything from the earthly (partying, sex, cars, death) to the spiritual (love, God, salvation, reincarnation). Some lyrics were intellectual, others bizarre. Some political, others just playful. Some insightful, others humorous. Some almost religious, others downright raunchy. One thing was for sure, they were never bog standard.

HIS MUSICIANSHIP - Prince was a skilled keyboardist, bassist, and drummer, but his forte was as a guitarist. His guitar solos were a show on their own – big, bold, flamboyant and dramatic with crying, wailing bends, speedy flurries of notes, moving from a peak only to climb to an even higher one. *'Purple Rain'* is the obvious example.

HIS SHOWMANSHIP – He was viewed by many as the consummate performer, with his endless energy and boundless creativity. He was probably the best overall dance mover I've ever seen live (at least equal to if not surpassing Michael Jackson). Everything he did; every gesture, step, movement seemed in perfect rhythm and flow, and whilst no doubt closely rehearsed, his shows retained a sense of fluid spontaneity.

Before his tragic untimely death in 2016 of an accidental overdose, Kirsten & I had the privilege of seeing Prince live in both 1988 and again in 1990 – both were completely different.

The first at Wembley Arena was a concert in the round. Kirsten and I had good seats but were at the back of the stage. Gigs in the round weren't supposed to have a back, but from memory we had more 'back' proportionally than the other side. But when our back did become the front, it was fantastic. The concert was in two halves – the first half was the more obscure funk found on the then newly released 'LoveSexy' album. The second half was non-stop hits, and they all flowed one after another like an unstoppable juggernaut - '1999', 'Alphabet Street', 'Kiss', 'When Doves Cry', 'Raspberry Beret', etc - brilliant(!) - plus there was that moment! [check out Appendix A:4]

<u>The second</u> was at the NEC Birmingham. This was a more traditional stage layout, and was a greatest hits show from start to finish. My clear memory here was an epic version of *'Purple Rain'* with an immense extended solo amidst full effects. Kirsten and I took a friend of ours to this concert, who was a big Prince fan, but who also happened to be our church Pastor's daughter. We were a little concerned over the raunchiness of some parts of the show.

I think she kept quiet - at least we were never reprimanded!

Chapter 38 – Brilliant Intellectual Madness
REM
De Montford Hall, Leicester 1989

'Rolling Stone' magazine in the late 80s published an issue with REM on the cover with the heading – 'America's Greatest Rock 'n' Roll Band', and proceeded to put forward a convincing argument as to why. Not bad considering their commercial and artistic peak hadn't yet begun.

I love REM. They have created a mountain of great albums stacked with huge pop and rock songs, yet always avoiding the predictable cliches. Just when you thought you had this band sussed, they take another surprising detour exploring new territory, which would be a little scary for the band's followers, were it not for the fact that the basic REM sound was always retained. The point is, you never not know its them, and that provides security because then you kind of know it's all going to be alright.

1989 was a watershed time for the band. 'Green' was the sixth REM album but the first with a new record label. This was somewhat of a controversial decision jumping from I.R.S. Records, an independent label that has championed underground acts, to big-time Warner Bros. Records. But REM knew what they needed to do to take them to the next step.

In my opinion, *'Green'* was their weakest album so far, certainly lacking the power and energy of the last record *'Document'*. But the Warner's 'machine' did its job regarding promotion, a big part of which included a huge 130 date world tour which lasted all year. By the end of it they were global superstars, and still the best was yet to come.

The *'Green'* tour is the only time I managed to see REM live. On this tour they successfully took on the challenge to fill the larger arenas, whilst at the same time not forgetting the smaller 'theatre' venues. So, for example on the UK leg, they played Wembley arena with a 12,500 capacity, but also De Montford Hall in Leicester, where I went, which only held around 2,000... which is probably why I was able to get to the front.

Opening with *'Pop Song '89'*, my favourite track off *'Green'*, examining the part pop music has to play. Is it for entertainment or has it a role to play politically? (*Should we talk about the weather? Should we talk about the government?*) R.E.M. answered with a series of blistering songs that provided wonderful entertainment for the night but pulled no punches in bringing to attention the corrupt dishonesty that exists in the highest corridors of power.

Front man, Michael Stipe is a fascinating character. He had a magnetism on stage - you simply can't take your eyes off him. He often acted out the songs with a series of unconventional movements — one moment he would be standing still, the next he would be moving or dancing across stage at a frantic pace like a man possessed. He was totally unpredictable and you are left with the dilemma of whether Stipe is a super intelligent genius or a complete fruitcake. The answer is probably both, but neither of these alters the fact that he is probably the coolest rock star ever to grace a stage.

Three songs off my favourite REM album '*Life's rich Pageant*' make me happy and to finish with, the sublime '*It's the end of the world as we know it (and I feel fine)*', with its fast-flowing list of lyrics, in the tradition of Dylan's '*Subterranean Homesick Blues*', which Stipe attributes to a stream of consciousness caused by TV channel flicking. [Proof of how much of this song's lyrics you can recite is a true indication of how big an REM fan you really are!!]

The band played their last gig in 2008. They followed it up with a final album in 2010 [*Collapse into Now*] and said 'Goodbye' with a final song '*Discover*' in 2011. They bowed out at the top of their game and are still as popular as ever.

After the show in 1989, I remember walking into the night air as a very satisfied gig-goer. On reviewing the gig some 25 years later, I realise that they are a band I really do miss, and have in my opinion left a huge hole in the rock scene.

Michael Stipe; Intellectual genius, cool rock star, and mad as a hatter

PART THREE
THE 1990s

Chapter 39
The UEA Gigs (1986 - 1992)
Norwich

From 1984, and until 1992 when we left for New Zealand, Kirsten & I were based in central Norfolk. The closest venue for regular gigs was the University of East Anglia on the outskirts of Norwich. We saw many concerts there. The trouble is that there was a period when tickets that were issued were just collected on the night and we had no ticket stub portion given back to us. No ticket stub meant no accurate record of gigs. So, whilst I have pieced together a list of the bands and artists we saw there during that period, I can't be absolutely certain I haven't forgotten any.

THE WATERBOYS 1986

I had seen this band support U2 at Wembley Arena in 1984 and they were so good, even today they are the enduring memory of that show.

The early Waterboys sound became known as *'The Big Music'*. This was due to both the vastness in sound brought about by brass and strings inclusion, and the grandeur of imagery in the lyrics. Mike Scott, the bands vocalist and frontman described it as "a metaphor for seeing God's signature in the world."

Scott is a complex and sometimes controversial figure, never afraid to experiment with the Waterboys sound. When a song called *'Whole of the Moon'* off the

'This is the Sea' album made the Top 30, he refused to go on *'Top of the Pops'* because it meant lip-syncing to a recording of the song rather than playing live. This hindered the band's promotion but that didn't seem to bother him.

The UEA gig setlist included several new folk and fiddle based 'raggle-taggle' style songs, which was somewhat a return to Scott's roots and provided a totally extra dimension. It was again a stunning performance, life giving and refreshing to the soul.

On the way out afterwards, I overheard a conversation a couple of guys were having about the show. One was commenting to the other about what a brilliant gig it was – but that it was a shame that they didn't play *'The Whole of the Moon'*. I followed them out thinking perhaps that was exactly why it was so brilliant! [40]

KATRINA & THE WAVES 1986

This was a fun gig and as I remember, a bit of a home coming gig for Katrina with her parents in the audience. Of course, everyone was there to hear *'Walking on Sunshine'*. Obviously, the band knew that because they played the song twice, once about half way through and an extended version for the encore. This was a 'happy' gig indeed and there weren't many people without a smile on their face as they left.

---

[40] I saw the Waterboys again in 2023 in Cambridge. 37 years on, they were just as brilliant, playing for well over 2 hours. This time they did play *'Whole of the Moon'* as well as a stunning version of *'This is the Sea'* and Prince's *'Purple Rain'* for the final encore.

John Otway (without Wild Willy Barrett) was the support I seem to remember.

HUMAN LEAGUE 1986

A very different kind of gig, with this popular band who are one of the best in the 'New Romantics/ synth pop' genre. Singer, Phil Oakey formed the band and there is the well documented story that he spent some time searching for a female backing singer. One evening in a Sheffield night club he spotted Joanne Catherall (the dark haired one) and Susan Ann Sulley (the blonde haired one) dancing and knew instantly they would be right. He approached them there and then inviting them to join. At 17 years old, they did!

There are clear memories for me of this evening. I remember

- Marvelling at how the full band plus the 2 backing singers managed to fit on the small UEA stage
- Thinking how tall singer Phil Oakey was, and how fortunate it was with the low ceiling that he was a sideways swayer rather than an up and down bopper.
- Being surprised how many songs I knew and how much I enjoyed this gig. They finished the set brilliantly with *'Together in Electric Dreams'*, *'Don't you want me?'* and *'Mirror Man'*

SQUEEZE 1987 and 1988

Two gigs in two years from this band from Deptford in South East London. I had seen Squeeze support 'The Police' at Milton Keynes but somehow the smaller venue suited the band. You know exactly what you're going to get with Squeeze and sure enough, *'Cool for Cats', 'Up the Junction', 'Pulling Mussels from a Shell,' 'Annie get your Gun,' 'Tempted', 'Hourglass'*... the list of singalongs go on – A predictable, fantastic night out.

GARY GLITTER 1987, 1988

See Next Chapter

THE MISSION 1988

Goth Rock Band who were touring promoting their second album *'Children'* and had just got chart success with the single *'Tower of Strength'*. A good solid performance with singer Wayne Hussey in good brooding form. Atmospheric rock at its best.

THE ALARM 1988/1990/1991

The Alarm are the ultimate anthemic, hands in the air, singalong rock band led by Mike Peters. Very much in the same vein as U2 and like them, seemed to be destined for super stardom. Unfortunately, band dynamics and factions prevented progress and they split in 1991, although Mike Peters continues to fly the flag. We had already seen them a couple of times in 1984 and 85, and here were three more shows in four years at the UEA, promoting albums *'Eye of the Hurricane'* (88), *'Change'* (90) and *'Raw'* (91).

with a catalogue of live favourites already in the bag (*'68 Guns', 'Spirit of 76', 'Blaze of Glory'*). Each show was full of energy and life, guaranteeing you left with sore throats having sung your heart out, and sore arms from punching the air. One of the best live bands to see.

CURIOSITY KILLED THE CAT 1988
Curiosity killed the Cat were a bit of a *"flash in the pan"* 5-piece boy band that hit the heights rapidly in the late 1980s and then disappeared equally quickly. They had a charismatic singer in Ben Volpeliere-Pierrot (complete with trademark beret) and a couple of good tunes in *'Down to Earth'* and *'Misfit'*.

Did I really go to this gig? I have the ticket but I have to confess, I can't remember a single thing about it!

ALL ABOUT EVE 1989
A fascinating band mainly due to the lead vocalist Julianne Regan, who had a stunning voice, a mysterious beauty and a moody personality. All About Eve were a folk-pop/rock outfit whose biggest hit was the haunting *'Martha's Harbour'*. Of course, some may recall the infamous incident on *'Top of the Pops'* when All about Eve performed this song. Well, I say 'performed'!!?? TOTP went out live weekly and the bands mimed the songs to backing tracks but, on this occasion, the stage monitors weren't switched on. This resulted in both the Studio and TV audiences being able to hear the backing track, whilst the band couldn't.

They sat motionless waiting some time for their cue in what was a truly embarrassing and cringable moment.

In all, this was a good gig. Despite the fact Julianne Regan seemed in a bad mood – no smiles or audience interaction apart from when she appeared to get annoyed with a couple of drunk people in the audience, storming off stage at one point.

Awesome end to the gig with an explosive version of the song *'December'* which is off the second album *'Scarlet & Other Stories'* involving an almighty extended solo by guitarist Tim Bricheno.

FISH – 1990
The first tour as a solo artist following the split from Marillion. This is still probably my favourite of many times I've seen Fish, and I cover this in Chapter 58.

HOTHOUSE FLOWERS 1990
Hothouse Flowers are another of those bands you can't help feeling never quite reached their potential. On knowing the band is led by Liam O Maonlai on keyboard and vocals, there are no prizes for guessing they are from Ireland. They got a helping hand from U2's Bono in launching their first single, but it was the late 80s when things took off following the release of their first album *'People'*, which became the most successful debut release in Irish history. I love this album with its blend of soul, gospel, folk and rock, creating a fresh, unique sound. This gig followed the second album called 'Home'. It was a fantastic night, full of energy and life with

notable great musicianship. The crowd were right behind the band and highlights were *'Don't Go', 'Movies'* and a brilliant rendition of *'I can see Clearly now'*.

AL STEWART 1991
Always up for a bit more Al! This time he toured with Fairport Convention's Iain Matthews. It was an acoustic show, contrasting with the full band gig back in 1984. Stand out memory on this one is that he played the classic *'Nostradamus'* in full.

BARCLAY JAMES HARVEST 1992
A much better gig than last time I saw them twelve years ago. For a start, there was a great support band called 'To Hell with Burgundy'. Then BJH played a great set with a lot of old faves starting with *'Mockingbird'* and ending with *'Hymn'*. They went down well but in the twelve years since I last saw them, they are still all music and little performance.

Chapter 40 - All that Glitters
Gary Glitter
Mallard Park Peterborough 1991

The first question has to be 'Why at the start of the decade of the 1990s is there a chapter on an artist that appears to belong in the heart of the 1970s?'

The simple answer is because I was still going to the concerts! This was the sixth and final Gary Glitter concert that I attended (not counting the one in 1994 that never was - c/f Appendix A:12). This had become a kind of ritual every Christmas - simply as a response to the fact that Gary was touring every December and it's interesting that I have probably seen GG with more gig going friends (i.e. a wider range) than any other artist.

Why so? Simply because without question you were guaranteed a fantastic party night out like no other, and when you'd been once and "got it", you wanted to be back next year. You see, every year was the same - the same gimmicks, the same songs, the same outrageous costumes but no one would have it any other way. The only slight difference was that both the venues and crowds grew bigger each year.

The extraordinary career of Gary Glitter began in the 1960s when Paul Gadd (real name) became Paul Raven. Despite being involved in numerous projects, they yielded only minor success. But with the birth of the glam rock movement in the early 1970s, Gadd adopted a new stage name, Gary Glitter [41] and things took off. With his backing group, 'The Glitter Band', he hi-jacked the charts with a series of singles, of which both *'Leader of the Gang'* and *'I Love you, Love me, Love'* hit the UK No 1 spot. To reinforce his image, he continuously 'glammed it up' reportedly owning thirty glitter suits and fifty pairs of silver platform boots. His fans loved it and he became affectionately known among them as 'The Leader'.

With the emergence of punk in the mid-late '70s the glam scene saw a rapid decline in popularity. Glitter's record sales had already started to wane, and it seemed there was no place for him anymore, forcing a decision to take 'early' retirement.

The post punk era seemed to bring with it a little more leniency and openness helped by the diversity of new wave. This provided the opportunity for Glitter to 'test the water'. So, in 1981, he cut a dance medley of his greatest hits, *"All That Glitters"*, which surprisingly charted.

And so, the revival began.

Starting with small venues, Glitter began to perform his OTT shows and a clear pattern emerged with those who attended.

Most went along to mock, scoff and generally take the piss, but rapidly realised that someone had beaten them to it. And that someone was Glitter himself. He had (as John Peel brilliantly described in a concert review) 'A keen sense of the ridiculous'. Adding alongside, a substantial back catalogue of equally ridiculous sing-a-long songs that

---

[41] Apparently, the name came about by playing alliteratively with letters of the alphabet, working backwards from Z. Other options considered included Terry Tinsel, Stanley Sparkle and Vick Vomit

most people knew, (but up until now probably would never have admitted it) seemed to result in a winning formula! So each individual who attended a gig seemed to experience a similar metamorphism. This stemmed from a dawning realisation, that the <u>whole thing</u> – from image to songs to show – everything was all tongue in cheek!

Instead of people standing on the outside laughing <u>at him</u>, they found that they could relax, enter in and laugh <u>with him</u>, and have a thoroughly fantastic time doing so. The result was a kind of popularity revival. Seedy cabaret clubs gave way to college and uni venues in the 80s and then concert halls and arenas in the 90s. His final show being a 7,500 sell out in Sheffield.

I first saw Gary Glitter in 1984 in the open air at Status Quo's Farewell Concert (c/f chapter 29) where he was the surprise stand out success proving that despite the diversity of location and venue, the formula still worked.

Turning to the 1991 Christmas Gang show gig in Peterborough. My memories of the evening are as follows:

The magic moment arrives when the house lights go out and the darkness is met by rapturous applause. Immediately, eyes strain through the gloom scanning the stage to catch first sight of 'The Leader'. The experienced among us know however, that there is probably at least 10 minutes introduction build up before that happens! Sure enough, we are treated first to the 1812 overture blasting out of the speaker stacks, accompanied by billowing spoke and thunder and lightning effects. Then the band appear launching into *'Rock n' Roll',*

GG's first hit which introduced us to the classic Glitter sound, with the crowd supplying ample support on the 'HEYS!' Then a spotlight picks out a figure in familiar pose with his back to the audience in full glitter attire. The audience erupts, the figure turns... <u>but it's not Him!</u> Then same deal on the other side of the stage and we suddenly realise we are being teased by a succession of 'pseudo-Garys', serving to push anticipation to frenzied levels. Then finally just as the song ends, appearing centre stage high up, another figure in full glitter costume with back turned. Is it Him? All we can see initially are the shoulder pads, the size of Bournemouth, but then he turns... <u>It's Him!!</u> Legendary pose and quiff a quivering. The crowd go bananas. He maintains the pose for at least a minute with no sound other than a couple of thousand people yelling. And you realise that before a word has been spoken and a note has been sung, that he has the whole 'gang' eating out of his hand! A lesson in the art of successful theatrics.

Then his first words greet us: *'Did you Miss Me?'* before launching into *'Hello Hello, I'm Back Again'*... and yes, we really had!

A couple of songs in, the jacket comes off in the first of several costume changes. A half open glitzy shirt reveals chest hair galore, which just seems to create more opportunity for posturing... all the time of course - he [as well as us] is totally aware of the complete silliness of it all. Hit followed hit, with Gazza flamboyantly strutting from one side of the stage to the other, scampering up ramps and back down again and stopping every now and again for yet another shameless pose (probably to get his breath back). But the best is saved for the encore as engine revs belt through the speakers, followed by Gary entering the stage on a huge Harley and we are treated to *'Leader of the Gang'* starting and finishing with the iconic *'Come on, Come on!'* singalong. What a show! Many came to scoff but all stayed to cheer and you can bet they will be back next year!

Glitter Confessions

I confess to a dilemma.

What do you do when an entertainer you really like does something really bad?

In 2015, Gary Glitter was found guilty of child sex crimes including molestation, sex and rape of minors. Add this to bankruptcy, drunk driving and previous convictions for sex offences, he ended up in prison for a 16-year sentence. Controversially in early 2023 Glitter was released from prison having served half his term, although he was subject to strict license controls. Yet within a few months he was back behind bars having been found to be attempting to access the Dark Web.

These horrendous crimes can easily lead to a variety of emotions, from a sadness to a revulsion. This of course leads to some important questions. If you're a fan, do you stop being a fan?

Do you stop listening to the songs?

Do you clear your record collection out?

Do you throw your concert programmes and ticket stubs in the bin?

Certainly, the media had a "clear out" with all radio stations united in not playing any songs and the BBC removing any clips from repeat 'Top of the Pops' episodes. But what about me personally?

Well, I confess I'm a bit confused.

Whenever I used to get together with fellow gig goers who had attended a Gary concert with me, you could guarantee that at some point in the evening that one of us would strike a 'Glitter' Pose, or quote a lyric, or simply reminisce and laugh. But since the conviction, there has been a general unease. Even mentioning a gig or a song would lead to an uncomfortable atmosphere, alongside a personal low-level sense of guilt with none of us knowing quite what to say or how to respond.

Yet, I can't erase the memory of the shows and great times we had. So, the questions keep coming.

Can you separate the theatrical onstage character from the real man? If so, is it right to do so? Does it make a difference if the legal system concludes that he has now served his sentence, and paid the penalty for his crime, and released him.?

And what if on release he chose to tour again?

Would you go? Could you go?

If only the answers were as simple to answer as the questions are to ask! Now it has to be on every individual's conscience in arriving at answers. For me, I don't think I ever would or could go again if there were future shows.

Yet at the same time, I cannot deny the memories and even the feelings of fondness of some amazing gigs from the past... but in the past they will remain!

Chapter 41 – Farewell Freddie
The Freddie Mercury Tribute Concert
Wembley Stadium 1992

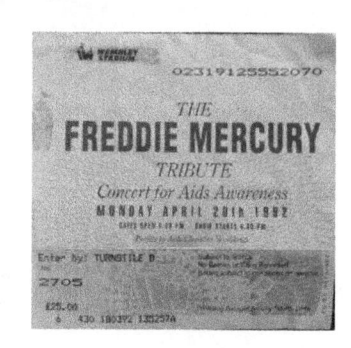

An enormous event as one of the greatest gatherings of rock stars ever assembled for one show, came together to pay tribute to arguably the greatest rock performer ever!

Never have I felt the need to be at a gig as much as I did for this event. So, when Brian May, John Deacon and Roger Taylor announced live on TV at the Brit Awards, that they were organising a special tribute show to be held at Wembley to celebrate the life and legacy of Freddie, I set my focus on nothing else but to make sure I got a ticket.

As I mentioned at the start of Chapter 3, no band has influenced my musical journey and given me such enjoyment over the years, and I just knew I needed to be there. Why? Nothing to do with the line-up of stars, but a variety of personal reasons: for closure, to celebrate, to mourn, to say 'thank you' and to be in a congregation of like-minded people who loved Freddie. It was fitting for me also that it was held at Wembley, the same venue as the unforgettable '86 gig, the last time I saw Queen.

It's impossible to cover the gig in detail but here goes:

While waiting for the show to start, I remember just having long periods of soaking up the atmosphere, regurgitating memories, reflecting, thinking and praying.

The concert begins with Brian May, Roger Taylor and John Deacon taking to the stage to welcome us and to invite us to join in with giving Freddie the biggest send off in history. With tears in our eyes, we agreed.

Four Bands did mini sets for the first half of the show – Metallica, Extreme, Def Leppard and Guns and Roses. Extreme's whole set was a medley of Queen songs.

From then on (the second half of the show) was Queen playing their songs with guest artists providing vocals for each one.

The list below shows the Queen songs performed, along with the artist(es) who performed them. I've also added (for a bit of fun) a personal ranking from 1 to 17 of each performance (i.e. from the sublime to the awful). This is a bit unfair because however far short an artist fell, they were carried by Queen, the occasion and the crowd, so even a poor performance still came over as a great song.

Nevertheless...

TIE YOUR MOTHER DOWN
Joe Elliot of Def Leppard   15

First song up led by Brian May, who was then joined onstage by Joe Elliot of Def Leppard. It wasn't the best suited song for him perhaps, but he did OK. Slash from Guns & Roses also came on stage to add guitar backing to Brian, whilst at the same time having an identical permed haircut as him.

I WANT IT ALL
Roger Daltrey of The Who   13

Roger's still proving he's got the voice (and the lion's mane perm). He ripped through the song and was a good match. However, he was still carried by the band which made him sound better than he probably was

LAS PALABRAS DE AMOR
Zucchero   8

One of Queen's lesser-known songs off the *Hot Space* album taken on by this Italian singer. Passionately performed and pitch perfect, taking the song further... great job.

HAMMER TO FALL
Gary Cherone of Extreme   6
Back into hard rock and an ideal song for the antics of Cherone who has already put in a good shift. Yet again a top-notch performance. Black Sabbath's guitarist Tony Iommi is also on stage at this point.

STONE COLD CRAZY
James Hetfield of Metallica   11
This match wasn't a surprise as Metallica had recorded the song two years previous for a record label compilation and ended up using it as a B-side as well. Hetfield's voice was at its gravelliest for this number played at a frantic pace.

INNUENDO/ CRAZY LITLE THING
Robert Plant of Led Zeppelin   17
If you wanted an artist to perform 'Innuendo', with its 'Zeppelin-esque' grooves and tones, you would look no further than Robert Plant. But this actually turned out not to be pretty. Plant couldn't hit the high notes, yet refused to give in trying, plus he lost his way once. The fact that he refused permission for the song to be included on the subsequently released DVD tells the story.

Similarly, 'Crazy Little Thing called Love' was a horrible mismatch. Don't get me wrong, the song went down a treat but it was the crowd choir and the band that made it so great. And I'm sure the 'Ready

Freddie' shout from the crowd could probably have been heard in Birmingham!

TOO MUCH LOVE WILL KILL YOU
<u>Brian May</u>   <u>3</u>

Brian, solo on keyboard, performing this beautiful song from 'Made in Heaven', probably saw tissue stock in the stadium deplete by 90%. Almost too much for the emotions to bear. Amazing!

RADIO GA GA
<u>Paul Young</u>   <u>9</u>

It would be hard to mess up such an amazing live song, and Paul Young, pop act from the 80s didn't. He performed it confidently with some twirly mic stand tricks, and carried it home.

WHO WANTS TO LIVE FOREVER
<u>Seal</u>   2

A stunning song, sung stunningly well. I remember being touched by this in 1986 and marvelling how Freddie used the slow build-up of the song to max effect in the stadium environment. Seal followed suit and delivered what was an incredibly sensitive, haunting, simple and soulful performance. Tears galore again! A lovely moment at the end when Seal after bowing to the crowd, turns and bows to the band in Freddie's honour.

I WANT TO BREAK FREE
Lisa Stansfield   7

Very well performed appearing with hairnet and curlers pulling a vacuum on stage (paying homage to the band's brilliant and hilarious *'Coronation Street'* take off video for this song).

UNDER PRESSURE
David Bowie & Annie Lennox   4

Next up is David Bowie, who of course collaborated with Queen on the original song back in 1981, hitting the No1 spot. Joining him on stage to sing Freddie's part is Eurythmics singer, Annie Lennox. The two deliver a touching performance with a nice ending. After this Bowie also performs 'Heroes', a fitting tribute.

SOMEBODY TO LOVE /39
George Michael   1

It stood out at the event, and seeing the concert on DVD afterwards confirmed for me, the stand out performance was George Michael singing *'Somebody to Love'*. Superb voice, bringing the best out of the song, full of energy working the crowd to perfection, and capturing the spirit and showmanship of Freddie like no one else on the day.

THESE ARE THE DAYS OF OUR LIVES
George Michael & Lisa Stansfield   5

George goes on to sing a duet with Lisa Stansfield that is a powerfully emotional version of Freddie's last song.

BOHEMIAN RHAPSODY
Elton John & Axl Rose   16

To play Queen's Magnum Opus needed something special. And valiant attempts were made. I think Elton was the perfect choice for the first piano part, and it was a neat idea to have the bouncing, spinning Axl Rose come on for the rock part. But for me it just didn't work. It would be vastly unfair to be critical and I don't want to be. Whoever took this song on would have found it a huge vocal challenge. Only the crowd could sing it to the heights it deserved, and we did! However, it must be said that seeing Elton and Axl duetting with arms round each other for the close of the song, surely has to be one of the more unusual sights in the history of rock music!

THE SHOW MUST GO ON
Elton John   11

Elton did much better on this one, clearly putting his all into it. He must have liked it as he included it in his live set for some time. Queen must have also liked it, including it on their Greatest Hits 3 album.

WE WILL ROCK YOU
Axl Rose of Guns & Roses   14

Axl returns for this iconic chant. He had the attitude but the crowd could have done it without him.

WE ARE THE CHAMPIONS
Liza Minelli   10

To finish off proceedings, came probably the most surprising performer of the night - one of a completely different pedigree from everyone else on the Wembley stage, movie legend Liza Minelli, a performer much loved and admired by Freddie. Whilst the anthemic masterpiece, 'We Are the Champions' was not really suited to the deep, cabaret voice of Minelli, no one really cared because no one really heard her above the vast unified vocal outpouring from every person in the stadium. After the second chorus, the entire cast of the show appeared on stage to help finish the song, say their 'goodnight' to the crowd and to join in with a final 'goodbye' to Freddie.

What a night! Of course, there were other key moments outside of the songs. Movie star icon Elizabeth Taylor came on stage to announce that proceeds of the concert would go to AIDS charities,[42] and David Bowie falling on his knees to *recite 'The Lord's Prayer.'*

---

[42] In fact, the proceeds of the concert went to establish the Mercury Phoenix Trust, a charitable organisation dedicated to fighting HIV/AIDS

This event was widely reported to have been the greatest gig of the 1990s. It is the most broadcast live concert of all time with 70 countries having shown the event live on TV creating an estimated worldwide global audience of one billion people. Fitting for the incredible line up that performed that day.

In hindsight, I have a real sense of privilege that I was there. I would not have seen David Bowie or George Michael play live if it had not been for this gig. In fact, that applies to the majority of the line up.

But really all that took a back seat, because in a sense, it came down to just me needing to be there for me, and that was enough.

As I look back now, I see it being probably the most important of all the gigs I've been to.

George Michael finds lots of bodies to love

Chapter 42 – Love is all around
Wet Wet Wet
Logan Campbell Centre Auckland 1995

Long time, no gig! So, I felt very thankful when this concert was announced. Kirsten & I had a soft spot for WWW. They had matured from a boy band into a mainstream pop band and their *'Picture This'* album was high on our playlist. We had a really enjoyable relaxed evening. Marty Pellow's voice was outstanding as in fact was the quality of the whole band. It was one of those performances where the songs played live completely echoed the recorded versions.

It's interesting that some gig-goers put high value on this. In other words, for the purists among an audience the closer the live song is to the recorded version that they know, determines the quality of the gig for them. The other side of the coin are the bands that tend to change the live version to make it different – a change in lyric, an extended solo, or a variation in melody, providing the potential of the element of surprise. I tend to generally fall into the latter category. However, this gig oozed quality and it was a joy to see a band comfortable in not only what they delivered, but the way they delivered it. Needless to say, we sung along to some pop classics such as *'Love is all around'* and *'Sweet Little Mystery'* and we left with a real sense of satisfaction.

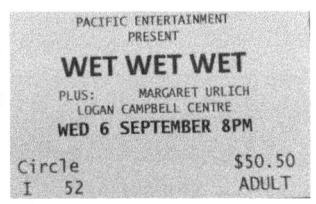

```
PACIFIC ENTERTAINMENT
       PRESENT

   WET WET WET
PLUS:    MARGARET URLICH
     LOGAN CAMPBELL CENTRE
   WED 6 SEPTEMBER 8PM

Circle              $50.50
I    52              ADULT
```

PART FOUR
THE 2000s

Chapter 43 – A Healthy Pile of Undies
Tom Jones
North Shore Events Centre Auckland 2000

You know you're in for a good night when you arrive at the gig venue and keep bumping into lookalikes of who you're there to see.

Tom Jones is an icon in the UK & US of course but if he had any doubts as to how well he would be received on the other side of the globe, he needn't have worried.

With the pre-concert yelling and screaming from the sell-out crowd, we could have been at Cardiff Arms Park and when Tom came on stage, he was greeted with not only wild cheering but an extended time of applause. How appropriate considering the rare dual identity he carries – the combination of the boy next door alongside the Vegas legend – and he was getting the respect he deserved.

The voice was as powerful as ever, and we were treated to his expansive octave range as he took us through the decades of hits including the soulful *'Keep your Hat on'*, the cheeky *'Kiss'* and the downright raunchy *'Sex bomb'* which he did twice!!

And yes, I can confirm the traditional salute of sexy underwear being brought or hurled to the stage by various ladies of differing ages is not only still happening, but growing. Certainly, the onstage pile grew throughout the show aided by a couple of pairs of giant bloomers.

Tom took it all in his stride, occasionally selecting a pair to mop his brow with. And I confess, when he started to belt out the singalong gems such as *'What's new Pussycat'*, *'Delilah'* and *'It's not unusual'*; they were so good, I could have added my own briefs to the pile!

A brilliant night!

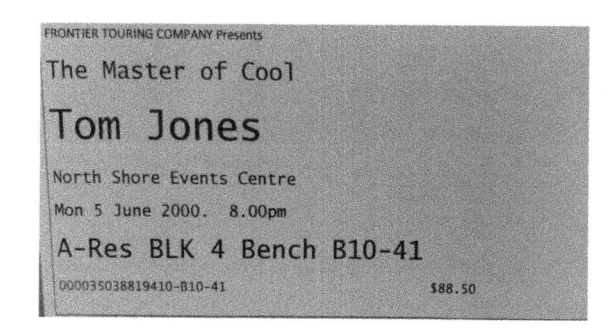

```
FRONTIER TOURING COMPANY Presents
The Master of Cool
Tom Jones
North Shore Events Centre
Mon 5 June 2000.  8.00pm
A-Res BLK 4 Bench B10-41
000035038819410-B10-41                    $88.50
```

Chapter 44 – The Art of Entertainment
Robbie Williams
Ericsson Stadium Auckland 2001

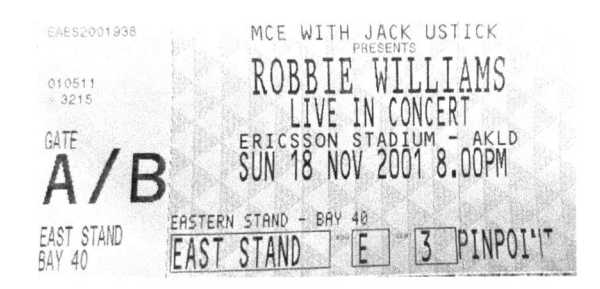

```
EAES2001938        MCE WITH JACK USTICK
                         PRESENTS
010511         ROBBIE WILLIAMS
  3215            LIVE IN CONCERT
GATE           ERICSSON STADIUM - AKLD
A/B            SUN 18 NOV 2001 8.00PM

EAST STAND    EASTERN STAND - BAY 40
BAY 40        EAST STAND   E   3  PINPOI'T
```

I had become a big fan of Robbie since his first solo record *'Life through a Lens'*, and then seeing his phenomenal Knebworth gig on DVD. So, when Auckland concerts were announced, it was a must.

I didn't realise it at the time but this was my first stadium gig for almost ten years. In fact, in the time living in New Zealand, I had only been to two gigs in that period. This showed the isolation of New Zealand both geographically and musically. I don't remember feeling I was missing out at the time, just cut off and unaware of what was going on. I realised this more after our returning to UK soil.

I went along with my best mate in NZ and also saw this as an opportunity to take my eldest son Ben, aged 10, to his first ever gig. A New Zealand band called 'Zed' who I really liked, were support. But they were soon forgotten as Robert Peter Williams hit the stage!

You can't help but love Robbie. He has an outrageous arrogance yet underneath it all is a simplistic innocence[43]. This dual persona seems forever present - the superstar showman Robbie, unreachable and untouchable, yet at times allowing a glimpse into his humanity revealing an innocent vulnerability, enough to want to cheer him on. And every time he appears to be stepping over the mark, he seems to pull it back just in time. He can be crude with lots of bad language, but the fact he's hyped up giving it all he's got for the audience (including you) somehow compensates in making it forgivable and him still lovable. I think as time has gone on, with maturity the arrogance is more part of the performance than real and it's all now very tongue in cheek – the best example is the song *'The Heavy Entertainment Show'* – check out those lyrics and I defy you not to at the very least break out in a wide grin!

Robbie Williams has to be one of the best entertainers to emerge in my generation. He has promised to entertain us! And he certainly did on this Sunday evening in Auckland. A huge atmospheric build up and then as the opening chord sequence to *'Let me Entertain You'* blasts out from the speakers, Robbie makes his entrance suspended high above the stage, dangling upside down from a bungie rope, mirroring the cover of the *'Escapology'* album. There is nothing understated about the start to the show whatsoever. Nor in fact for the rest of it! A cover of Paul McCartney's Wings Bond Song *'Live and Let Die'* follows

---

[43] I remember at the end of the Knebworth set, him looking into the camera and mouthing 'Did I do OK?' To which every viewer responded (in their hearts at least) 'Yes you really did Rob!'

and then a barrage of Robbie classics (*Strong, Supreme, Kids, Rock DJ*). There are a few cheeky references to 'Take That' (during *'No Regrets'* and a punk rock version of *'Back for Good'*) and inevitably *'Angels'* to finish.

It was great to see my son up, dancing and enjoying the gig so much. However, there is training to be done – I need to educate him that you do <u>not</u> request to go to the toilet during the encore cover of Queen's *'We will Rock You'* and *'We are the Champions'*!

It was a fantastic gig and much superior to the O2 gig in London that I took my younger son to some ten years later. The gig here was in the round. My son loved it but I was disappointed. Our seats were high up and both visually and audibly it was under par. There was however a surprise appearance by Gary Barlow who by this time had patched up differences with Robbie and they did a couple of duets, with Gary on the piano. And of course, *'Angels'* overrides any good seat/ bad seat issue. I mean you could be blindfolded in the car park and it would still be phenomenal.

Robbie Williams - knows how to make an entrance

Chapter 45 - Comparisons
Delirious?
Waterfront Norwich 2001 & New Zealand Parachute Festival 2002

A visit back to the UK for Christmas 2001 and a trip to see our Norfolk friends coincided with an opportunity to see Delirious? play in Norwich as part of their 'Tension' Tour. Well, you can't turn down opportunities like that, can you?

Now it just so happened that I also had plans to see this band headline New Zealand's 'Parachute' Festival, the largest Christian event of its kind in the Southern Hemisphere, a few weeks after our return to NZ. Twice within two months on each side of the globe.

I loved Delirious? They were a band that almost single-handedly restored my hope that the message of the Christian faith could be naturally and freshly proclaimed through great rock music.

So it was exciting to me to see the same band playing a smallish venue of around 700 capacity followed by an outdoor large stage gig in front of 25,000, with 12,000 miles in between. To me, this was an interesting exercise in comparison. How would the band fare with the different size stage, crowd, and sound system as well as being in a different country, continent and hemisphere? I also wondered from the band's point of view, what it must have felt like to play such a diverse size of audience. And which

I wonder is more nerve racking? To play to a vast sea of unidentifiable people? Or to see eyeballs in front of you?

From my point of view on the gig-goer's side of the fence (barricade), all I can say is both shows were exceptional. The comparison aspect was harder than I thought, because it feels like you are seeing a different band. This is due to the image the venue portrays. Being up close brings a gritty realism – you are aware it's five guys on stage that have practiced a lot, but they are human and you still hear the wrong note. Whereas in a large venue, observing a band from a distance can seem like you are observing a product or a package. However, if I had to pick a favourite out of the two, I would go for the festival gig – for the reason that Delirious? songs suit a large arena/stadium. Take *'History Maker'* for example – there's few better singalong anthemic songs. Even the recorded version is brilliant, but put it in a live context with several thousand people and it becomes explosive!

And it was one such night in New Zealand. Although obviously jet-lagged, the band received a traditional Māori welcome on stage (the haka and nose rubbing) before launching into their set with the amazing *'Deeper'*, growing in energy and life the more the set went on.

I left enriched with the reminder that singing out lyrics that express your faith in a large gathering somehow makes God seem bigger and the world seem better.

> **The Union of UEA Students**
> FURIOUS? RECORDS PRESENTS
>
> # DELIRIOUS?
>
> **plus Special Guests**
>
> Thursday 6th December 2001
>
> **The Waterfront**
> 139-141 King Street,
> Norwich
>
> £10.00 Adv.
> (Subject To Booking Fee)
> More On The Door
> Doors 7:30pm
>
> **P.T.O.**   **OVER 14'S ONLY**   **00005**
>
> Right of admission reserved. Box office info 01603 50-80-50
> Ticket may be subject to a booking fee.   Conditions overleaf

Faith Confessions

I confess I am a Christian believer. I have been since 1982, although for some of those early years I hardly walked the walk. But from as early as I can remember, I have always had a deep-seated belief that God existed in some form. I have never been able to get past the fact that by looking and contemplating the wonder, diversity, beauty and vastness of the world and universe that we inhabit, such intricacy of design and order, simply must have a designer behind it all.

The likening of my faith to a journey is very appropriate, always moving, lots of twists and turns, stops here and there along the way, sunshine and storms, and discovering new vistas. The result is that where I am now in my thoughts, beliefs and questionings seem a million miles from where I started from. And of course, I know there's more to come as I've kind of sussed out you never *'arrive'* as such, at least not in this life.

Music has and continues to play a vital role in my faith journey (and I know I speak for many), especially from a desire to connect with and express myself to God. Whilst I love some of the old hymns, my preferred style of worship has been contemporary with modern songs played on modern instruments.

Living in New Zealand for much of the 1990s and into the new millennium, I saw the emergence of two large churches, both in Sydney – *Hillsong* and *Christian City Church*. Both have been hugely influential globally in the areas of praise and worship, breaking new ground and attracting many of the younger generation back to churches.

But what of the 'secular' music scene? I recall debates back in the 80s as to whether or not a christian should listen to non-christian music? (I shudder at the thought). It's kind of ironic thinking back that one of the reasons why I continued to listen and enjoy 'secular music' was that there was little alternative that was decent. The main stream christian scene seemed dull to me. I remember listening to several 'christian' bands trying to find something that was alive, but constantly found cliched mundane formulaic music with little imagination. Therefore, I rejoiced when in 1997, I heard an album called *'King of Fools'* by Delirious? Here was a refreshing new sound, unpredictable creative songs, brilliant riffs and lyrics that clearly spoke of a faith that was connected with real life. It was (dare I say) 'spiritual' as opposed to 'christian'. The other thing I really liked about this band was they didn't opt for the safety of the 'christian bubble'. They entered the mainstream music scene without compromising the message of love and hope, and very effectively too, supporting bands such as Bon Jovi and Bryan Adams along the way. [It's interesting that whilst many of their songs are sung in church services even today, when the band decided to call it a day in 2009, their final performance was not in a church, but a sold-out Hammersmith Apollo]. I so admire them and many other artists (e.g. Bono & U2, Alex Band & the Calling, Mike Peters & the Alarm, Mike Scott & the Waterboys) for bringing spiritual songs to the mainstream rock circuit. It's not easy but it is needed. And it's obvious that the power and success of all the above examples, is because their music has simply been a reflection of their lives.

Chapter 46 – A Design for Life
James Dean Bradfield
Koko, London 2006

Being away from the UK for 14 years, I had some catching up to do in the 'gig' department. Settling in East London would give me plenty of opportunity. My first excursion turned out to be James Dean Bradfield. Since I had been overseas, one band I had really got into was the Manic Street Preachers, a solid rock trio from Wales who kept bringing out quality record after record, and they were high on the list to see. Whilst I had to wait a little while longer to see the band, here was the next best thing. Frontman James Dean Bradfield doing a tour on the back of a solo album *'The Great Western'*.

I had not been to 'Koko' before. A nice venue – smallish theatre size with about 1400 capacity. Built in 1900, its past has had many lives: the Camden Hippodrome Cinema, A BBC recording venue (the Goon Show was recorded here), and then as a music venue opening as 'The Music Machine' in the 70s ripe for punk gigs and then changing to Camden Palace in the 80s for the new romantic onslaught. It became Koko in 2004 after extensive refurbishment, following a fire. [44]

I was at the front in the circle for James Dean Bradfield and a mention is needed for Vega 4, the

---

[44] Koko has in the 2020s had a further £70 million refurbishment and is now not only a gig venue but a whole complex including recording studio, radio station, roof top restaurant, library and cocktail bar.

support band, one of the best I've seen. They gave out free demo CDs with sample tracks on, and because of this I ended up listening to them quite a lot subsequently. Good marketing!

Bradfield delivered a great show starting with *'Emigré'*, one of the best songs from his solo album. In fact, the set was mostly new album, interspersed with some Manics tracks including a brilliant version of *'All Surface No Feeling'*. We also got an acoustic version of *'A Design for Life'* which was one song I really wanted to hear live. And very appropriate too. I found tonight so life giving and refreshing, and realised how much I'd missed that feeling of energy and vitality. It seemed to blow the stale cobwebs away and get me firmly back on the 'gig-going' highway.

Chapter 47 – Reading it Wrong.
The Feelers
Shepherd's Bush Empire London 2007

How ironic that after living in New Zealand for fourteen years, it is not until I return to the UK that I get to see my favourite kiwi band live - The Feelers; their album *'Playground Battle'* was a favourite of both mine and my son, Ben. When I saw they were playing at 'Shepherd's Bush Empire', I was not only surprised but was keen to check them out.

So, on a dreadful cold and wet February evening, Ben & I traipsed across London. To be honest I wasn't expecting much – Shepherd's Bush Empire was a 2,000 capacity venue and my assumption was it would probably be half empty - I mean who would come out on a horrible winters night to see a fairly obscure kiwi band?

Well, I confess I had read it completely wrong. I obviously underestimated the kiwi contingent that tended to be strongest around this part of London. I also underestimated the popularity of 'The Feelers'. The show was sold out, the venue packed and buzzing.

The Feelers are not the most charismatic of performers, but they are no-nonsense, straight down the line rock, with great songs. 'Venus' and 'Larger than Life' stood out and it was well worth the haul across town.

Chapter 48 - London with Benefits
Linkin Park
Astoria, London 2007

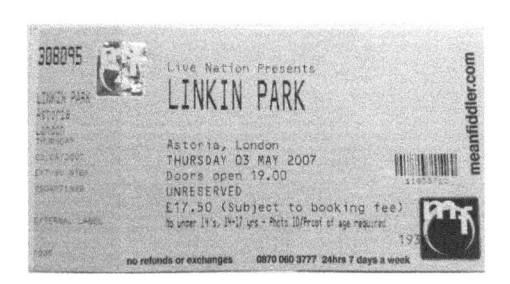

Linkin Park was Ben's favourite band, so when they announced a last-minute addition to their sold-out arena tour – I landed two tickets on the actual day of the gig (such is the benefit of living in London). It was an intimate concert at the *'Astoria'* - part promo show, and part warm up gig. I didn't tell Ben until he got home from school. I don't think he believed me until we were in the venue itself.

It had been three years since Linkin Park last played in the UK. A long running dispute with their record company was now resolved. They were happy! The crowd were happy (endlessly chanting the band's name). The mood was euphoric, the atmosphere electric. The fuse was lit!

Linkin Park were deemed an important outfit from the aspect that their 2001 *'Hybrid Theory'* put nu-metal firmly in the mainstream. The formula is successful – Chester Bennington is the main vocalist, an amazing voice that diversifies from a melodic, angelic whisper to a murderous, spine-tingling scream. Then there's Mike Shinoda, the rhythm guitarist who puts the rap into the band's rap-rock, and all this is backed by aggressive guitars and thunderous, swarming rhythms.

Whilst a little heavy for me, this was a phenomenal show, as LP ripped through a range of songs from old faves to (what seemed like slightly more commercial) new material. Bennington was wild - regularly straining to hi-five the grabbing hands of the mosh pit, with two worried security men battling to keep him from being pulled in and devoured. '*Numb*' and the superb '*In the End*' finished off the evening, and the band departed as heroes. As I've said before, there's nothing like seeing a big band play an intimate venue. There is a sense of privilege wrapped up in it all.

There is however a sadness as I look back.

Firstly, the Astoria, an iconic venue is no more. It closed in January 2009 following a compulsory purchase due to the government's Crossrail plans.

Secondly, also Chester Bennington is no more, a victim of depression, he ended up taking his own life in 2017. We and the world mourned yet again a tragic, futile loss of a talented life, who had it all, yet was unable to handle what that meant and, in the end, left us way too soon!

How long to sing this song?

Chester Bennington at the Astoria. 2 great Losses

Chapter 49 – Cultivated Canadians
Simple Plan
Electric Ballroom, 2008

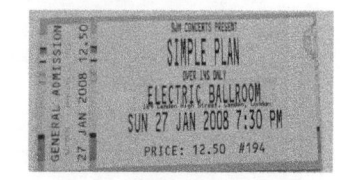

This Canadian pop-punk band had a knack of penning songs that connected with the teen issues and problems of the day. In 2011, they wrote an amazing track called *'This Song Saved My Life'*. The lyrics were based on real correspondence the band had received over the years, from fans who testified how the lyrics of their songs had literally saved them in their battle with inferiority, rejection, loneliness and suicide contemplation. [Who says there's no power in music?].

Simple Plan were fantastic at this sold-out gig at the Electric Ballroom in the heart of Camden. It was packed tight and we couldn't get anywhere near the front and settled for a position about half way back. They were promoting their excellent third album called *'Simple Plan'*. These songs were aired amidst a great atmosphere.

A great moment of 'light relief' in the show was when vocalist Pierre Bouvier (being French Canadian) addressed the audience in French. Immediately somebody from the crowd yelled back a response in French. Pierre was obviously surprised he got a reply back in his own language and retorted with a grin on his face, "Hey you Londoners are so cultivated"...

Of course, he meant to say 'Cultured' –

How ironic was that?

Chapter 50 – Legends Line Up.
Childline Rocks
Indigo O2, London 2008

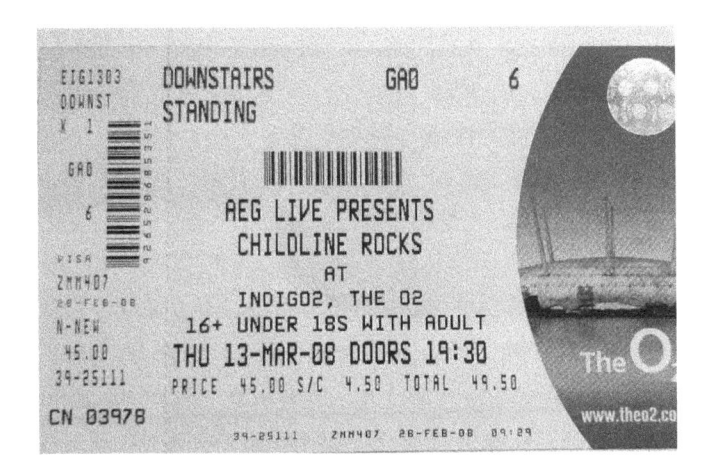

My first ever charity gig, held at the O2 Indigo. Ben & I went along because Fish was on the bill, along with Marillion. An historic reunion perhaps? In fact... no it didn't happen, but it turned out to be a great night, with a number of legends from the rock industry, including the show's host/compare for the evening – radio's 'whispering' Bob Harris. The format was simple, that each artist did three to four songs.

THUNDER opened the show. I hadn't heard them before and they were great. Good commercial melodic rock heard live, always goes down well to fresh ears.

FISH did a couple of songs off *13th Star* and *'Incommunicado'*, a Marillion Song. Stormed it!

MARILLION with 'new' singer (well eighteen years old new) Steve Hogarth. They were OK but I didn't know any of the songs.

THE ZOMBIES had their heyday in the 1960s. It's rare to proclaim these days that a band were 'before my time' but these guys really were. I had heard of Colin Blunstone and Rod Argent but wasn't familiar with any songs, until they played *'She's not there'*, and I realised this was one of these bands that you knew a few of their songs but didn't know who it was who sung them.

RUSS BALLARD joined the Zombies on stage. The original band split in 1969, and went on to form 'Argent' whom Ballard played guitar for. *'Hold your Head up'* was their big hit which got the crowd going tonight.

DEEP PURPLE or at least two of them. (Vocalist and guitarist Glenn Hughes and original drummer Ian Paice) came next with two DP songs, a rousing version of *'Mistreated'*, and *'Might just Take your Life'*

LULU was a surprise guest and actually stole the show with the best performance of the night with an extended version of *'Shout'*, working the crowd like a true legend. I mean, come on – who's going to steal the show in a line up featuring classic rock acts with an audience who are predominantly serious classic rock fans? A female pop star from the 60s? Never in a million years, well... except perhaps one Thursday evening in March '08!

ROGER DALTREY was the official headliner with Thunder returning as his backing band. Three 'Who' songs followed including *'Behind Blue Eyes'* and *'The Kids are alright'* before bringing everyone back on stage in traditional charity gig style, for an encore performance of *'With a little Help from my Friends'*

So, in all – a satisfying night. Added to the fact that you never quite knew what was going to happen next (which created an ongoing tension), we were in the company of some true iconic legends of British rock and pop, and had a rather good time too!

Chapter 51- Elvis ain't Dead
Scouting for Girls
Shepherd's Bush Empire
London 2008

'Scouting For Girls' are one of the top acts to emerge from the new millennium, and very different from any band I've heard before. They comprise of a trio of mates from the same school - Roy Stride (keyboards and vocals), Greg Churchouse (bass & vocals) and Peter Ellard (drums) - who were inspired by REM's *'Out of Time'* album and decided to start a band. Two years later in 2007, they released their self-titled debut album which turned out to be a classic – full of instantly memorable, life-affirming, singalong indie-pop songs. They are above all a fun band, whose songs deal tongue in cheek with stories of teen angst, and the longings, fantasies, and losses of those early relationships. The clever, cheeky lyrics have a strange combination of making you smile, whilst at the same time resonating a deep, maybe even a sub-conscious reality in the fact we've all been there. I mean who hasn't wanted to be *'James Bond, just for the day?'*

The concert at Shepherd's Bush was great entertainment if not a bit wild at times. Kirsten was with me for this gig and we had standing tickets, but even positioning ourselves to the side, I had to protect her a few times from the moshing of an extremely enthusiastic crowd. They played their entire debut album and thanks to Roy Stride's constant encouragements, we left with hoarse voices that had endured a high-level workout.

Everyone says the biggest challenge of producing a brilliant first record is following it up. It's very rare for a band to come even close, and it has to be said Scouting for Girls join the throngs in never hitting those early heights. But you know, twenty or so years later, and with seven albums, two million record sales and four Brit award nominations behind them, the original three schoolboy mates, Stride, Churchouse and Ellard are still going strong, still selling out tours and still producing great songs.

Elvis ain't dead indeed!

Chapter 52 – A Tangible Warmth
Keane
Shepherd's Bush Empire
London 2009

In 2009 one of the most significant independent record labels, Island Records, celebrated their fiftieth anniversary. To celebrate, they hired out the Shepherd's Bush Empire and put on a week of gigs featuring their signed artists, both established and up and coming. It was a great line up over the week with headlining acts each night that included Amy Winehouse, Paul Weller and Cat Stevens (now Yusef.) That's how I got to see Keane, who headlined on the Saturday night (with support from TomTom Club)[45]

I had wanted to see Keane for some time. Their outstanding debut record *Hopes and Fears* had become a firm favourite of mine.

The first noticeable thing to say was that I have never experienced such a warmth generated by an audience to an artist. It was a tangible feeling of love and appreciation conveyed to Keane. Whether it was to do with vocalist Tom Chaplin's battle against addiction that was now public knowledge, I don't know. But it was extraordinary, and the band responded. They played a great show and Tom's voice seemed as pure as could be. But this was a strange gig for me, because for some unknown reason I felt out of sorts. Rather than

---

[45] U2 made a guest appearance one night – sadly not mine.

entering in, it was like I watched from the side lines, feeling a bit like a neutral spectator. I don't know why - it wasn't the band and it wasn't the songs and it certainly wasn't the atmosphere. It was just one of those nights when I struggled to feel a part of it all.

The following week I saw myself briefly on TV which aired a compilation of the week's gigs. In the one second I was on screen, I thought I looked to be enjoying it!

PART FIVE
THE 2010s

Chapter 53 – Knobheads arise
The Brit Awards 2010
Earl's Court London

What a great way to start off a brand-new decade by participating in a brand-new experience – Kirsten & I attended the 2010 Brit Awards. Neither of us had ever attended anything like an award ceremony before, nor had we been part of a live TV Broadcast so it was somewhat of an unorthodox gig to get the 2010s rolling.

The Brit Awards are showcased in an event to recognise the best in British popular music. It first took place in 1977 as an initial 'one-off' linked in with the Queen's silver jubilee. It's significant then that this year's awards were held at Earl's Court bringing back memories of that first visit in that same year.

The next Brits ceremony happened in 1982, and it was from then on that it became an annual event. 2010 marked the thirty year celebration, so the producers worked hard to make the occasion a little bit special. Our ticket instructions were that we had to be seated in the auditorium by 7.45pm for an 8pm broadcast time. Our seats were in one of the vast banked areas around the arena, and the floor was set up like a gigantic restaurant with tables for the stars and guests. We were all set to go:

THE START
A spectacular opening as Lily Allen descends onto the main stage on top of a Space Rocket performing '*The Fear*'.

THE WARNING
Peter Kay the comedian hosts the show, but his intro speech is far from humorous, warning nomination presenters and award winners to keep it short and calling for an evening of 'responsible fun'.

THE KNOBHEAD
The above was totally ignored by Liam Gallagher, who collected an award for the Oasis Album '*What's the Story Morning Glory*' and then arrogantly in some sort of protest, threw both the award and the microphone into the audience. Peter Kay's response made it on air a split second before the programme cut to a commercial break: '*What a knobhead*'!

THE COMMERCIAL BREAKS
The advert breaks on the live TV broadcast were essential moments for adjustments to the sets & transition to the next part of the show. This was (and had to be) managed to the micro second. After the flurry of activity, we were counted down (from ten to zero) heralding the resumption of the live broadcast.

THE PRESENTERS

There was a notable array of stars reading the nominees for each category and presenting the awards. These included Shirley Bassey, Noddy Holder, Courtney Love and two fifths of the Spice Girls, Geri and Mel B.

THE WINNERS

The main winners on the night were boy band, JLS and rock diva, Lady GaGa. Both performed live. JLS were lowered down on wires as the entry to their performance. Lady GaGa's song was new but to be honest it was hard to get past the white lace outfit, the substantial headdress making up in material for the what the rest of the garment lacked.

THE DUETS

Two outstanding duets raised the bar of the evening. Dizzie Rascal teamed up with Florence and the Machine in a brilliant version of *'You've got the Love'*, but even better was Jay Z's collaboration with Alicia Keys to perform *'New York State of Mind'*. The power in Key's vocals were out of this world. When she hit a power high note, it seemed like the structure of Earl's Court moved.

THE FINALE

The Finale was the reason we got tickets in the first place. Robbie Williams was awarded the outstanding contribution award, and closed the show with a fifteen minute medley of his greatest hits. A 'WOW' moment, worthy of attendance alone. What a special evening and experience.

Chapter 54 – Soft Spot
Squeeze
Indigo 02 2010

I don't know anyone who's been into music since the 1970s that hasn't got a soft spot for Squeeze. Chris Difford and Glen Tilbrook have been together longer than Batman and Robin it seems, and the great thing is it shows. They are so tight and confident now, with a commanding stage presence generated through years of gig experience. Tilbrook's vocals are as clear and distinctive as ever, and the energy and love for what they do is still totally evident. The set list was fantastic and despite virtually all the songs being from the last century, would we have expected or indeed wanted anything else? A totally fun evening. Oh yes - almost forgot to mention The Lightning Seeds were special guest support, and rather good they were too.

Chapter 55 – The Child Prodigy
Joe Bonamassa
Hammersmith Apollo 2011

I was invited to this by one of my gig-going companions from uni days. I knew nothing of Bonamassa other than he was supposedly one of the world's best blues rock guitarists. He was in fact a child prodigy, playing guitar at age four, mentored and trained by American guitar legend Danny Gatton at age eleven and had his own band by twelve years old, which ended up opening for BB King.

Well, it was no 'opening for' anybody else this evening. The hardworking Bonamassa performed two and a half hours of virtuoso guitar work to this sold-out venue for the second night in a row. It was a quality gig and easy to see why he is considered by many to be the best guitarist of our generation. His variation in style from rock to blues to gentle acoustic picking to wonderful lead solos – he is master of all. Of course, his backing band is top notch too, notably the man behind the kit, Tal Bergman, who is simply one of the best drummers I have seen. There was some great interplay between the band and moments when they would try to outdo each other, which lightened the mood, providing a contrast with the intensity of some songs.

I didn't know much of the setlist, although it was well stocked with a number of cover versions of musicians who have inspired and influenced him. So the start of the show was a song called *'Cradle Rock'* a tribute to Rory Gallagher, followed soon by *'Midnight Blues'*, a Gary Moore cover, then later ZZ Top's *'Just got Paid'*, and a duet with his (then) partner Sandi Thom performing Leonard Cohen's *'Bird on a Wire'*.

Of his own material, the track *'Sloe Gin'* was one I knew but the highlight was a song I didn't know – the set closer called *'Mountain Time'*, with a sublime guitar solo at the end. This has since become a regular on my playlist.'

The next four chapters cover four artists that I saw several times in concert, the run of gigs which were centred in (although not exclusive to) the decade of the 2010s

Chapter 56 – Bands on the Run 1
Coldplay

A band I had been desperate to see for some time. Coldplay had a formula that just worked. Their songs were getting stronger and their shows getting bigger. It was two years since arriving back in the UK that I first started this run of gigs.

1. O2 London 2008
The last night of three at the O2 celebrating the release of the album *'Viva la Vida.'* This was an early birthday present from Kirsten and our tickets were on the Arena floor. A great spot to enjoy a spectacular show, which included large bouncing balls over the audience, butterfly confetti sprayed out to the point of drowning and a great light show. There was also a guest appearance by actor Simon Pegg who jammed along to a couple of acoustic numbers. *'Clocks'* and *'Fix You'* were stand out tracks.

Coldplay – First Sighting 2008

2. O2 London 2011

Following the disappointment of the Michael Jackson shows the year before (c/f Appendix A:12), I was keen to find an alternative, memorable debut gig for my younger son. I figured Coldplay would be a safe bet, and I was right. It turned out to be perfect!

The great thing about the O2 is the approach to the arena from the Tube. From coming up the escalator, it's a bit like arriving at a futuristic city with the large dome of the O2 lit up and cylindrical towers serving as large pixelated screens advertising the show and other upcoming events.

This was the *'Mylo Xyloto'* tour and so *'Paradise'* and *'Charlie Brown'* got their first airings alongside the older classics. A highlight was that on entry, we were all given wrist bands to wear, which at several points during the show, sprung to life, emitting flashing lights which throbbed in time to the music. 20,000 wristbands exploding into life at the same time created a truly memorable moment. [c/f Appendix A:4]

3. O2 Indigo London 2016

Coldplay were down to open the Brits Awards in 2016 held in the O2 arena, and I discovered that on the same night, they were doing a last-minute late Charity gig (for 'War Child') in the much smaller 'Indigo O2' venue after the awards. The opportunity to see the biggest band in the world in an intimate venue was irresistible and somehow (I can't remember how!) I got a ticket. It was weird going into London late at night and arriving at the O2 as the audience for the awards were just starting to depart in all their posh glam outfits.

It was a long queue outside the Indigo and a long wait once inside, but eventually sometime after 11pm, on came Coldplay. I was fairly close to the front and the overriding feeling I got was how ordinary they were. I don't mean by this that they weren't good, but suddenly they were four normal blokes that walked on stage, picked up their instruments and played. I referred to this in Chapter 45 seeing Delirious? in a small venue, and once again I was reminded that so often with the big arena and stadium shows, the effects and lighting appear to the audience as a package with the band, and you are witnessing something that's not quite real.

But in this setting, a couple of blatant wrong notes, a false start – it was all very human – and in a sense, it could have been anybody.

Having said all that, it wasn't just anybody; it was Chris Martin, Guy Berryman, Jonny Buckland and Will Champion, who had something beyond the norm, a unique chemistry, a wealth of experience and the ability to write some very good songs. They rattled through eleven of them in this gig including *'Yellow', 'Clocks', 'Viva', 'Hymn for the weekend'* and *'A Sky full of Stars'* to finish, with *'til Kingdom Come'* (from the *'Amazing Spiderman'* movie) as an encore. The show still included some toned-down effects including some 'star' confetti blown into the audience (to keep the cleaners happy).

But this was a 'stripped down' Coldplay revealing four human beings showing a degree of vulnerability alongside a greatness. [46]

4. Wembley Stadium 2016

What a contrast to the last show. A packed Wembley Stadium for this 'Headful of Dreams' tour, and to be honest, the environment Coldplay belong in - no holds barred and no restrictions regarding stage effects. Coldplay certainly do 'spectacular' very well with the combination of laser lighting, pyrotechnics, cameras zooming over the crowd on wires and a massive stage with huge screens. From here a thirty metre runway led to a small stage on the end, on which Chris Martin spent some time running to-and-fro, engaging the crowd en-route.

We stood at ground level amongst the crowd which meant we missed out on some effects but it was a magnificent gig, full of vivid colour with a real sense of joy and life. It just made you feel great, and such was the buoyant mood amongst the crowd, the walk back to the tube amidst the throngs was actually rather enjoyable.

---

[46] I love how Dave Grohl describes meeting an icon in the flesh. *'When the one-dimensional image, becomes a living breathing, three-dimensional human being, it fills your soul with reassurance that even our most cherished heroes are flesh and bone.'* (From his 2021 memoirs 'The Storyteller' published by Simon & Schuster)

Wave Confessions

If you have been to any stadium concerts (or large sports events) since the mid 1980s you will probably have had the experience of being part of the Mexican Wave. I confess over the years of gig going, I have loved it and hated it (often both on the same occasion).

Now just in case you don't know what I'm talking about, this phenomenon (according to the Oxford English Dictionary) is "An effect resembling a moving wave produced by successive sections of the crowd in a stadium standing up, raising their arms, lowering them and sitting down again".

It caught on globally during the 1986 Football World Cup held in Mexico, (hence the name), although it was evident in the US at sporting events several years prior to this.

The first time you are part of 'the wave', it is quite something. It usually gets going with a small section of the crowd standing up and raising their arms accompanied by a loud shout. The noise then attracts the attention of the nearby sections of the crowd who then join in, increasing the volume level and before long the whole stadium (or indoor arena) is involved.

So, you can see it on the opposite side of the venue to where you are seated, gradually coming round, and then it's on your side – you can no longer see it but you can sense it approaching; you can hear the noise coming towards you which gets louder and louder and suddenly it's on you like a tidal wave, you're up off your seat with a loud cheer and back down again, as it passes by.

And that first time it feels great. After all, you are part of something communal that is visually impressive, and yes, the fact that it worked and is still happening is partly down to you. A satisfying boost to the ego.

However, there is a very familiar pattern which involves a deterioration in emotional wellbeing!! And it happens in stages:
STAGE 1 – The stage of Full Enthusiasm - It's new, it's fresh, it's exciting. You feel part of something bigger, a sense of oneness with everyone else. As the noise of the wave approaches, you join in and with a crescendoing *WhooaahhHH*, leaping out your seat with maximum effort, both arms aloft.

STAGE 2 – The stage of Mild Irritation - This may be down to the length of one wave that keeps circulating or the frequency of new ones being generated. You respond with effort, but have the niggling sensation this is going on a bit too long.

STAGE 3 – The stage of Disturbed Comfort - You are starting to feel the effort of getting up from your seat too frequently. You continue to play a part but it's somewhat half-hearted – arms partially extended and a quick 'Whoa' partially raising from the seat you would much prefer to remain in.

STAGE 4 – The stage of Increasing Rebellion - You have all but lost interest. When the wave passes by, you no longer make any effort to get up from your seat, you may flip a hand loosely in the air, and any noise emitted is usually a kind of grunt, a few seconds after it has passed.

STAGE 5 – The stage of 'Don't give a Monkeys' - You no longer care... you just want the damn thing to stop! You remain seated with arms folded as a rebellious act of defiance.

These days the wave is not so common, but it still happens. I confess I would love to give it a permanent wave Goodbye!

Chapter 57 - Bands on the Run 2
Frank Turner

I was introduced to Frank Turner and his band, The Sleeping Souls, when watching the opening ceremony of the London Olympic Games in 2012 (I know I wasn't the only one). Organiser of the event, Danny Boyle, who was a fan of Frank Turner, asked him personally to do the crowd warm up. The song *'I still Believe'* was performed to an estimated 80,000 in the stadium and a further 25 million around the globe on TV. That song is still probably my favourite FT song but as I discovered, there were many other songs that were just as good, with a variety of styles from punk to folk to pop/rock, all great singalong material. Consequently, Frank has become a firm favourite of mine ever since, especially live.

I love the fact that he numbers his shows. It kind of gives an emphasis on the uniqueness of each one. The run of Frank's shows are as follows:

1. Forum London 2013 (Show 1384)

The first live show was with my son, Ben. We were upstairs on the balcony, which had really comfortable tiered cushioned seating, but the design made it great for standing too. My overriding memory of this gig was when Frank played the brilliant song *'Recovery'*, encouraging everyone to bounce. The balcony was full and I swear you could feel it moving. It would be an exaggeration to say it was like jumping on the end of a diving board, but that was the kind of feel; it was on this evening that I made an irrational promise to Ben that if his band ever headlined the 'Forum', I would do a stage-dive!

Well, they have since played at the Forum, but as a support. Whilst I wish them every success, a regular feature of my prayer life is they won't EVER headline the Forum

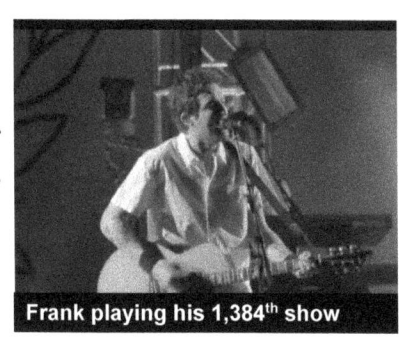

Frank playing his 1,384th show

2. O2 London 2014 (Show 1527)

A rare occasion because Kirsten & I, Ben & Dom all attended this gig together. It was a special one for Frank too, headlining the O2 which, with the exception of the Olympics, was his biggest show to date. He had two supports, both well-established. One was an English folk singer called *'Beans on Toast'* who performed and then later appeared on our block to watch Frank's set.

Second was an Irish American punk rock band, 'Flogging Molly' – a raucous outfit with great songs which seemed to be along the lines of drunken sailors and what you do with them.

Frank was fired up for this one and despite more swear words than not, he gave it everything. Starting with *'Photo-Synthesis'* and finishing with the excellent *'Four Simple Words'*.

3. Royal Albert Hall London 2015 (Show 1655)

This was a charity gig - part of an annual week-long series of gigs supporting Teenage Cancer Trust, organised by the Who. I took Dom having picked up tickets late through the Albert Hall resales. They turned out to be great seats close to the stage. Scottish band 'Idlewild' provided adequate support.

It was kind of neat that Frank opened tonight where he left off at my last show with *'Four Simple Words'*

4. House of Vans London 2016 (Show 1926)

One of the more unusual gigs: firstly, this was a free gig, with all tickets balloted, and I was successful in getting a couple. Secondly, *'House of Vans'* was a venue incorporated within a maze of tunnels underneath Waterloo Station. Ben had been here before, which was great because not only did he know roughly where to go, but also had I been on my own, I don't know how safe I would have felt. Dimly lit, graffitied tunnels with pockets of people sitting slouching and crouching against the walls, smoking something, and some eyeballing you as you went past. Once inside the venue, we followed smaller passages until it opened out into a bigger area. The stage was located at the end of a larger tunnel branch. There was also a photographic exhibition by Ben Morse celebrating eight years on the road with Frank, located in a smaller passage.

This was an acoustic show, but the amazing thing with Frank was that he has a voice that is so full, he could make a song sound like it had instrument accompaniment. A quick intro and welcome to show no. 1926 and then straight into *'Prufrock'*. The two hour set was brought to a conclusion by a medley of six songs, one from each of his albums. Exquisite !

5. Alexandra Palace London 2019 (Show 2309)
It's worth mentioning that it was in 1979 that I saw Queen at this venue, and the disorganised entry to the venue has not improved in the forty years since then. Unnecessary queuing and an entry system that was completely unfathomable in its method of operation.

Nevertheless, this was a much-anticipated gig, not least because the support was Jimmy Eat World. After the fabulous Troxy gig, I was almost looking forward to them as much as Frank. But what a disappointment. They were like a different band, not really connecting with the audience and delivering, in my opinion, a poor setlist of songs. A huge contrast with the show in 2016 (See Chapter 67). But Frank and The Sleeping Souls didn't let us down. Back to full band and introducing material from *'Be More Kind'*, we were pounded with a relentless set stuffed with classics galore.

6. Hyde Park, London 2023 (Show 2788)

Supporting Bruce Springsteen. The first time I'd seen Frank having the job of winning over an audience. It was a mid-afternoon forty-minute set, so not an easy challenge. But one he met well, endearing himself to the crowd by (i) choosing a good selection of songs for the occasion (ii) doing an extensive 'meet and greet' run through the audience and (iii) sharing that in his twenty five years of gigging and 2788 shows, to be invited to play alongside the Boss was the greatest honour.

Frank, I think you just won some hearts!

Chapter 58 – Bands on the Run 3
Fish

Outside of Queen, Fish has been the most important, influential and loved rock act in my life. The successful rise of Marillion in the late 1980s sadly also led to a strong difference of opinion between band and singer, leading to an inharmonious split. At the fork in the road, I went the Fish path following his journey as a solo artist, which has been somewhat bumpy over the years. Yet all credit to the big man, he stuck at it and received critical acclaim for his final album 'Weltschmerz' released in 2020. I simply never grow tired of listening to his music. He is a genius lyrically and always very poignant.

1. UEA Norwich 1990
Still probably my favourite Fish gig. His first solo tour introducing his debut album masterpiece, 'Vigil in a Wilderness of Mirrors', and it had everything.

As to be expected, most of this album was played, opening with the wonderful brooding title track, 'Vigil'. I find this album fascinating. It is as fresh today as when written. It is also prophetic in nature with lyrics to songs like *'State of Mind'* more relevant today than ever.

> I don't trust the government, I don't trust alternatives
> It's not that I'm paranoid, it's just that's the way it is
> Every day I hear a little scream inside. Every day I find it's getting louder.
> We the people are gettin' tired of your lies.
> We the people now believe that it's time
> We're demanding our rights to the answers
> We elect a precedent to a state of mind
> I trust in conspiracies, in the power of the military.
> In this wilderness of mirrors here, not even my speech is free
> We the people want it straight for a change
> We the people are getting tired of your games
> If you insult us with cheap propaganda
> We'll elect a precedent to a state of mind
> Every day I hear a little scream inside
> Every day I find it's getting louder…

In between the Vigil tracks were Marillion songs including *'Forgotten Sons'* as an encore; the power and emotion poured into this song at a level I have rarely seen equaled. (c/f Appendix A.5)

2. Oval Norwich 1992

I remember this gig was 'my last hurrah' just before our departure to live in New Zealand. I queued up to get a poster signed after the gig and asked Fish if he had ever played New Zealand / Australia. 'No, I'd love to,' he replied, 'it's just too expensive to take a show out there'. Just as I suspected! On this night, Fish was promoting *'Songs from the Mirror'*- an album of covers, and so the live set was mainly material from his first two albums and covers (including T. Rex's *'Jeepster'* and Bowie's *'Five Years'*) plus the Marillion trilogy of *Kayleigh, Lavender* and *Heart of Lothian'* as an encore.

3. Shepherd's Bush Empire London 2007

Fast forward fifteen years in the blink of an eye (so it seemed) after the New Zealand years. Now with ten albums under his belt as a solo artist and a new one released entitled *'The 13th Star'*. Tracks from this were blended with a selection from Marillion's *'Clutching at Straws'* celebrating its twentieth anniversary. Ben came with me, who wasn't even born when it first came out!

4. The Peel, Kingston upon Thames 2010

Fish embarked on a long tour called the Fishheads. These involved low key, stripped-down acoustic shows in smaller venues.

The Peel was a tiny venue – Fish emerged from the bar to get on stage, opening with a stunning acappella version of *'Chocolate Frogs'* before being joined onstage by guitarist, Frank Usher and keyboard player, Micky Simmonds, who treated us to a series of reworked songs, including a few never played in an electric set.

5. Islington Assembly Hall London 2017

6. Islington Assembly Hall London 2018

The tour in 2017 was supposed to be a showcase of the new album *'Weltschmerz'*, combined with the thirtieth anniversary of *'Clutching at Straws'*. Fish announced at the start that the album wasn't ready and there would be no *'Weltschmerz'* songs, but we did get the whole of *CAS*.

As a fairly last-minute arrangement, Ben & I went to the 'repeated' tour in 2018 with some new songs now included. The highlight was when Fish engaged in rapport with a female audience member, and as a request, did an impromptu version of 'Lavender'. A magic moment!

7. Live stream from Glasgow 2021
A Christmas show live streamed following lots of cancelled gigs. The first time I paid for a live gig without being there. So, I dimmed the lights, turned up the volume and watched from my sofa. The next best thing under the circumstances of COVID.

Will this be the future though?

I think the answer is yes and no. In many ways it is happening. And I suppose it's good to be thankful for the miracle of technology. The fact that I could 'be in the audience' in my very own living room is kind of neat. It also gives a fan the opportunity to see their favourite artist on the other side of the globe for example.

But nevertheless, it is always going to be second best to being there. No technology, however good, can be a substitute for the atmosphere, smells and sensations of a live gig.

NB: Fish will undertake a final 'Road to the Isles' Farewell tour in 2025. I have to be there!

Chapter 59 – Bands on the Run 4

Manic Street Preachers

It was fitting back in 2011 to celebrate twenty five years as a band that The Manics performed a special concert at the O2 and released a singles compilation entitled 'National Treasures'. Because that is exactly what they had become. And now, well into their second quarter century together with fourteen studio albums behind them, that reputation has only grown. This fiercely patriotic band from Wales have become a Great British Institution. There is something immensely reliable about the Manic Street Preachers. They are a firm favourite live band for so many including myself simply because you know what you're going to get:

- Good, solid, no-nonsense, intelligent rock with insight yet mystery and angry protest yet tenderness.
- Great vocals, wonderful guitar riffs & a bouncing circle dance from James Dean Bradfield
- Outlandish outfits, gangly dance moves, and a coarse rant from bassist, Nicky Wire.
- Solid, dependable rhythm from drummer, Sean Moore
- A plethora of great songs.

Homage to the band's guitarist, Richey Edwards missing since 1995, presumed-dead.

So, my run of gigs is thus:

1. Roundhouse London 2009

2. Roundhouse London 2011

Two gigs at the Roundhouse in Camden. The first was to promote *'Journal for Plague Lovers'* album. The whole record was played through in the first half and after an interval, a greatest hits set, starting with *'Motorcycle Emptiness'* and finishing with the superlative *'Design for Life'*

Bradfield @ 2011 gig

The second was with Ben who won free tickets as part of the i-tunes festival. A top setlist starting with *'You Love Us'* and finishing with *'If you Tolerate this,'* plus selections from the new *'Postcards from a Young Man'* album. A fascinating band by the name of 'Dry the River' supported.

3. Royal Albert Hall London 2016

Standing close to the front at the Albert Hall. A fantastic night. Anniversary tour of *'Everything Must Go'* played in full. Good support from 'The Editors'.

4. Corn Exchange Cambridge 2021

A great show with new material from *'The Ultra Vivid Lament'*. This was my first gig following the end of COVID lockdown and there was a sense of relief, gratitude and celebration, all around that normality appeared to have returned.

There was also a special moment when unexpectedly they played a track called *'Ocean Spray'*. Ocean Spray is a cranberry drink given to patients in hospitals in the UK and I knew this song was about James Dean Bradfield's mother and her battle with cancer. As my own dad was dying from blood cancer at this time, this song took on a new dimension of meaning. *"Oh, please stay awake and then we can drink some Ocean Spray"*. A pool of grief in the midst of a sea of joy.

Chapter 60 – Can't Put My Finger on it
Athlete
Shepherd's Bush Empire London 2013

I was aware that I seemed to be paying more and more visits to the Shepherd's Bush Empire. It certainly was one of the current "in" venues to play for bands on their visits to the capital at this time. I'm not exactly sure why - maybe it was the design where internally, height overshadowed depth, which resulted in it being a 2,000 capacity venue that could still retain a sense of intimacy.

For me however, this was not a favourite place. It was not so much the actual theatre but rather the location and my journey to get to it. It involved a bus or car to South Woodford in East London followed by a long, tedious pilgrimage of about twenty stops on the central line to Shepherd's Bush over in the west. However, the banality of the journey always seemed to be overshadowed by what awaited at the destination - and that was particularly the case for this gig.

Before a review however, a little about Athlete, who are/were an unusual band. They had a brief spell of activity over about six years releasing four albums including the excellent *'Tourist'* in 2005, which included a top five hit with *'Wires'*. They then seemed to go into semi-retirement, emerging occasionally for a festival or small anniversary tour. (This gig was a tenth anniversary for their debut record 'Vehicles and Animals').

Sadly, the band have now been AWOL for several years, which is a travesty. I say that because when I look back at my gig-going history, this concert is immediately up there in the ranks of the best. Like many bands, I still listen to their songs regularly, but unlike many bands, they kind of 'remain in me'. I think about them a lot and have strangely developed a warmth towards them, which (taking a phrase from one of their songs called 'El Salvador') 'I Can't quite put my finger on it.'

I have been thinking long and hard as to what it was that made this gig so impacting and have come up with the following thoughts:

- First there were some TOP 3 moments (See Appendix A sections 5 & 6)
- The variety of song styles and accompanying emotions were astonishing. For example, there is the powerful melodic rock of 'Half Light', the beauty of 'Rubiks Cube', the cheeky humour of 'You got the Style', the heart rendering emotion of 'Wires', the fun singalong of 'El Salvador', the captivating simplicity of 'Chances' and the spiritual hope conveyed in 'Black Swan Song'...and I could go on...
- The ability of vocalist Joel Potts to charge each song with the emotion it deserved, which had a highly contagious effect among the crowd.

- An overriding tangible humility from the band.
- It was clean, fun, life giving, uplifting, warming, intoxicating and wholesome — no bad boy rock stuff here — and all the better for it.

Athlete's appearances have gone now from few and far between to non-existent over recent years. It's a shame as I suspect I am one of many that regularly scan the new gig announcements in the fleeting hope that maybe, just maybe - it's time for a swan song.

Chapter 61 – The Edge
Kodaline & Dry the River
Forum, London 2013/14

Two 'new' bands who were attracting lots of interest, both held gigs at the Forum a few months apart. I attended both.

The first were Irish band, 'Kodaline', particularly being hyped with their first headlining tour promoting their debut album *'In a perfect World'*. And it seemed to be almost a perfect gig, except... now this was interesting. Something was missing here - but what? Fantastic catchy songs, good musicianship, beautiful vocals by Steve Garrigan, lovely harmonies, top quality sound, a singalong gem (*'All I Want'*) to encore with. It seemed to be all there! And yet...

it wasn't until I was halfway home when a thought occurred: 'an edge' – yes that was it, that's what was missing! That unexplainable, indefinable, something that can mean the difference between good and great.

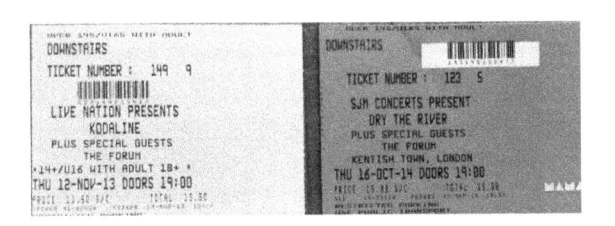

No such problem with 'Dry The River'.

I had first encountered this band supporting the Manics at the Roundhouse in 2011. Never have a band left me so temporarily confused. They were so different I wasn't sure if I loved them or hated them. They had an edge alright; I just wasn't sure if it was too sharp for me. Seeing them play without any prior knowledge left my mind grappling with songs containing both moments of unconventional weirdness yet clearly moments which reached heights of soaring power in which I felt my soul moved. And that is mostly the clincher. When my soul is moved, it usually turns out all good.

And it did. In the weeks following the gig I listened to the new debut album, *'Shallow Bed'*, which was a refreshing experience. Subsequently I've read various attempts by music journalists to describe the music style on this record: *"indie folk'"*, *"gothic rock drama"*, *"A bit Elbow, a bit The National, a bit Doves"*. But these all fall well short. In truth, they are like no one else, and it's a brave man who tries to place a label on them.

That's why this gig was so good for me. I was now familiar with both songs and the style. I could relax and enjoy without having to analyse, ponder and question. As a result, I found myself getting caught up in the show almost to new heights – particularly during the song *'No Rest'* which (like several of their songs) starts gently and then builds and builds to a robust, rapturous finale.

The main responsibility for the unique sound must fall in the lap of vocalist, Peter Liddle. He has a light almost choir boy warble which compliments the biblical and historical narrative in much of the lyrics. The soft undertones can turn into a powerful, piercing purity which matches the rising crescendos of the songs. Liddle is an interesting character in many ways. Tonight's gig was a flagship show. Not only had their second album *'Alarms in the Heart'* just been released but the headlining of this venue in many ways represented six years of hard work and graft to get to this point. Yet Liddle seems hugely uncomfortable with any sort of adulation, and tends to shy away from any limelight. On this night he seemed keen to get off stage at the end following a quick bow.

Maybe this was a contributing ingredient to the sad fact that in the following year, the band folded, leaving a significant legacy of five hundred plus shows in around fifty countries and a host of dedicated fans. The official citation for the demise was 'rough economic times'.

It's feasible this show may turn out to be the pinnacle of the band's history. If so, I consider myself fortunate to have been there.

Chapter 62 – Innocence & Experience
U2
O2 London 2015

I had seen U2 once at Wembley in 1984 where they were outshone by support band the Waterboys. Who would have thought we'd be turning up here thirty years on, to see them perform again, still as one of the biggest rock bands globally, performing a show of immense imagination and inventiveness that was a spectacle extraordinaire.

We had standing tickets which meant that on entry to the arena we could go right up to the 'stage', which actually stretched from one end of the arena to the other. In essence it was a performance 'in the round' except it wasn't in the round, it was more like a gigantic cat walk with a stage area at both ends.

No support tonight! With the elaborate stage show engineered, there's simply no room.

The lights go out as Patti Smith's *'Power to the People'* blasts over the sound system. Then Bono appears at one end of the catwalk under a searing spotlight to rapturous applause. He immediately engages the crowd, and then begins a journey across the catwalk, his walk breaking into a run and as he reaches the other end, the other three members of the band come into the light... and there we have U2 - complete, and without further ado, they power drive into a new song: *'The Miracle (of Joey Ramone)'*. A brilliant start !

No doubt about it, U2 carry something! There's a presence, a depth, a chemistry. And just as the coming together of a right combination of chemicals can create an explosive reaction, so too these four individuals when they come together as U2, create a unique dynamic energy. And after forty years, this has become very recognisable – you know what you are going to get. Yet despite the familiarity, a sense of cutting edge is still very much evident. Innocence and experience combined, hence the tour name. No better is this illustrated than about four songs in, and Bono announces 'a new song for today' and the band explode into *'I will Follow'*, the opener from 1980's debut album *'Boy'*, still as vibrant and fresh as ever, with the Edge's guitar riff piercing the auditorium atmosphere.

The innovative digital technology is impressive. The catwalk area between the stages incorporates two giant projector screens and these play an important role in the narrative aspects of the show, which represent chapters in the band's lives. For example, in the song, *'Iris (Hold Me Close)'*, Bono's interacts with his late mother through moving images. In *'Cedarwood Road'*, he walks down the street he grew up in, and we get to see and experience what that was like. Then *'Sunday Bloody Sunday'* relives the IRA bombings and grim images of Ireland at war. It was all very clever.

Having said all that, we missed much of the big screen effect by being positioned right at the front by the stage, (although great for a close up of Bono's shoes, every time he sauntered past).

What we didn't miss was the close of the set – *'Where the Streets have no Name', 'Pride (in the name of Love)'* and finally the haunting *'With or Without You'* which was stunning live.

Encores: *'City of Blinding Lights'* and *'Beautiful Day,'* and finally to finish the song *'One'* – the song that brought the band back together in the early 90s after a near split up, and tonight, a final song that unites both band and audience in a celebration of togetherness.

An epic, pulsating experience of a gig!

Bono searching the O2 for the rest of the band

Chapter 63 – Rhythms of the Night
Imagine Dragons
O2 London 2015

What a treat – two shows in three nights at the O2 arena. Following U2 was Las Vegas band, Imagine Dragons, who had risen to fame swiftly following their 2012 song, *"Radioactive.'* This song in many ways encapsulated the distinctive 'I.D.' sound – an upbeat, pop rock characterised by driven guitar riffs backed by a colossal rhythm and drum beats.

Indeed, all around the stage were large drums of various shapes which at times during the show were played in unison to create a gigantic reverberating beat adding power to the songs. Charismatic lead singer, Dan Reynolds spent some considerable time up and down the long 'runway' protruding from the main stage into the audience. During the songs he was dancing and interacting with the crowd, and in between songs he delivered numerous monologues expressing deep gratitude for the support of the fans. If you weren't one of the loyal faithful at the start of the show, you'd be hard pressed not to be one by the end.

There's a 'thing' I've noticed about gig-going. Some gigs may not create a huge impression on you on the night, but have more of a lasting impact. Others are immensely enjoyable on the night but don't 'last' quite as much in the future. For me, this gig fitted nicely into the second category. A fantastic concert and great night out, but it's not a band I listen to or think about that much.

Chapter 64 – A Lucky Escape
Enter Shikari
Alexandra Palace London 2016

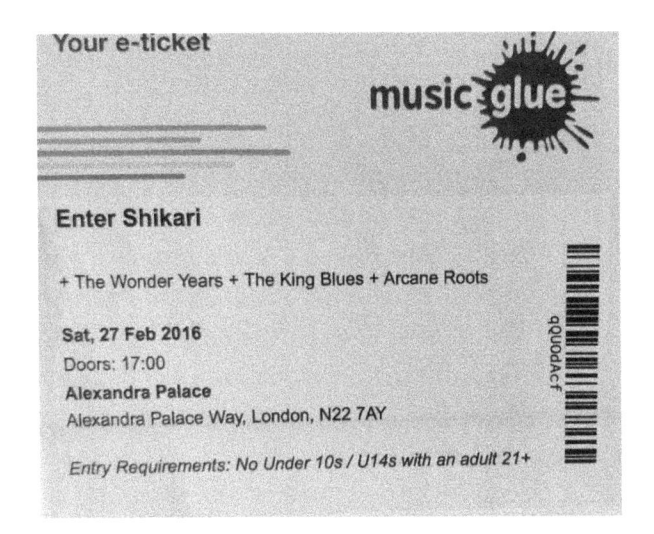

Your e-ticket

music glue

Enter Shikari

+ The Wonder Years + The King Blues + Arcane Roots

Sat, 27 Feb 2016
Doors: 17:00
Alexandra Palace
Alexandra Palace Way, London, N22 7AY

Entry Requirements: No Under 10s / U14s with an adult 21+

As you've gathered, I've always wanted my two boys to love live music and experience the live gig. It's always nice to get payback on an investment - well most of the time. For this gig my son, Dom, took me (well I really took him, but he really took me) to see 'Enter Shikari'.

'E.S' are a rock band who have been going since 2003; known for their crossover style fusing hardcore, heavy metal, and different electronic genres. This was a big gig for them and they pulled off a 10,000-crowd showing the extent of their following.

After a fiasco queuing to get in (once again - c/f chapter 57 part 5), we got ourselves a good place to see Arcane Roots, the first support band of the night, and another favourite of Dom's.

As it got closer to Shikari's set, you could feel the tension growing and the crowd swelling. There was pent up energy in the house and it felt like it was going to explode. I could tell serious moshing was on the cards. The question was 'Would I be far enough back to avoid it?' My answer came almost immediately. I felt a push on my back causing me to stumble forward. I turned round to see what was the cause, and there was a huge bald headed 'gentleman'(?) with a Shikari t-shirt which framed numerous tattoos on his large, muscular arms. He gave me a manic smile which was a kind of 'Are you up for this?' I wasn't! I was in fact contemplating my immediate future, the main priority of which seemed to be at this very moment to get out alive! I did not want the cause of death on my certificate to read "crushed by 18 stone crazy person". At that moment the lights went out, the crowd started to go wild; I seized the moment and ducked down, weaving my way out of the main crowd to the hopeful safety of the side lines. It was a good move. As soon as the band launched into opener, 'Solidarity', circle pits opened up in half a dozen places. From my vantage point I could see one of them was exactly where I had been and yes, '18 stone crazy person' was leading the charge. It was a lucky escape.

Enter Shikari were without doubt, loud and proud, and there were some great moments. '*The One True Colour*' was a standout song, and half way through the gig, vocalist, Rou Reynolds took to a second stage in the middle of the hall to perform 'Dear Future Historians', an uncharacteristic gentle piano number. Add to this an impressive light show and the result was a top gig, despite the fact that it was a bit metal for me. Undoubtably a memorable night that I wouldn't have missed. Plus, I was introduced to a great band, 'The King Blues', also on the bill as a support, who I still listen to today.

Health Confessions

I confess I have Parkinson's disease.

It was first diagnosed back in 2006, but I obviously had it several years prior to that because I went to a doctor when certain symptoms began to manifest, such as a tremor and foot dragging. The Doc thought it was benign and advised I drank Guinness (seriously!) I obeyed (naturally!) and it even seemed to work for a while. Yet sadly, it turned out to be a misdiagnosis. [Nevertheless, he still is my favourite Doctor ever!]

PD varies from person to person. 20 years on, I have come to realise I am extremely fortunate that the progression of my disease is unusually slow. This means that despite deterioration, I am still able to do many things I shouldn't be able too. Such is the strange, unpredictable nature of Parkinsons, making it often one of the less severe debilitating, neurological diseases. Someone I met recently likened his recent PD diagnosis to 'winning the world's worst lottery.'

My slow progression may be partially due to having the disease so young in life (or what is termed 'young onset'). However, I also suspect my love for music may have played a part too. There is no cure (yet) for Parkinson's, but it is widely accepted that music-based therapy programs improve functional mobility, fluidity and balance in patients with PD. On looking into this I have been amazed at how many studies have been undertaken, research experiments performed and books that have been written on the subject.

Whilst specific treatments vary (e.g., some believe in specific musical genres, others encourage humming, some dancing, some conducting, some chanting, some rhythmic drumming) but the common denominator is that there is power within the field of music to make positive change.

So how does it work? What is the music-brain connection?

In his book *'The Mozart Effect'* [Avon Books 1997], author Don Campbell puts it like this: *"The nervous system is like a symphony orchestra with different rhythms, melodies and instrumentations that keep the brain synchronised. So, when any part of the brain is damaged, the natural rhythms of brain and body are disturbed, and the neurons may fire at the wrong time or not at all. Often external music, movement or images help bring the neurological music back in tune."*

Alex Kerten's approach in his book *'Goodbye Parkinson's, Hello Life'* [Divine Arts 2016] is to use musical exercises to 'retrain' your body's movements replacing the chaotic tremors with a solid rhythmic structure. One exercise is to put on a favourite piece of music and enter in by becoming part of the band by letting your body be an instrument. I love this exercise – it finally gives me a valid excuse to go wild with an air guitar!

But it's not just Parkinsons of course. Music has been proven to benefit our general health in a variety of ways. Clinical tests have shown that music can contribute positively by reducing stress, blood pressure and symptoms of depression whilst, boosting creativity, motivation, memory and productivity. Hence, over recent years music therapy has moved from an area of scepticism to being widely embraced and now offers a valued career pathway in hospitals, rehab units, clinics, prisons and schools. The power in music is finally being acknowledged to the degree it deserves, offering real hope for tomorrow for many.

Chapter 65
Jimmy Eat World
Troxy, London 2016

OK, so here's a good one. When you go to a gig and it turns out to be special, how much of that is down to you? What I mean is we often focus on the band, or the performance or the effects - in other words what comes at us. But what about what comes from us? How much does that play a part? The reason I say this is that this gig by Jimmy Eat World at the Troxy is in my top gigs of all time, but the factors that place it there aren't what normally make a gig special.

Don't get me wrong. Jimmy Eat World were brilliant, the venue was excellent, the set list was near perfect plus they surprisingly played '23', one of my favourite songs.

But two others factors loom large.

The first factor was to do with my health. This gig came at a time when I was starting to find my Parkinson's affected my gig-going to the extent that my strength and endurance levels varied. Sometimes mid-gig, my limbs would be sore and stiff and I'd have to sit down. But on this night, it didn't seem to affect me. My energy levels were high and there was this moment when I found myself in the crowd close to the front, singing my heart out to a 'Jimmy' fave - moshing with all my strength totally lost in the moment and reveling in such a sense of freedom.

The second factor was that I was there with both my boys, a rare occasion considering the ten-year age gap. So not only was I able to enjoy it to the full, but I was able to enjoy them enjoying it to the full too and just for that one night, I was aware, I was awake, I was alive to the fact that I was sharing an experience right then, right there in that moment, and within it all was pure joy!

I have never quite experienced anything like that in a gig before or since. It seemed like a gift given to me just for that night, and one that lives on.

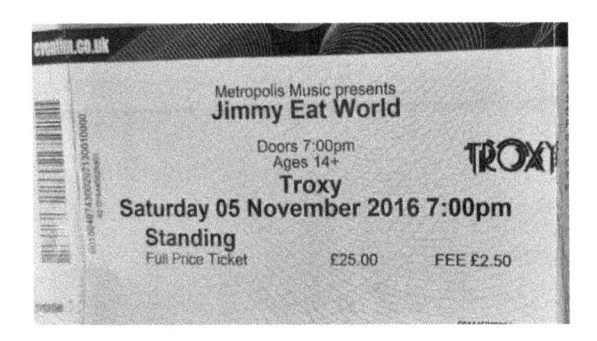

Chapter 66 – Good to be There
Tom Chaplin
London Palladium 2017

The first of two gigs this year at the famous London Palladium. Of course, this theatre was known as the home of variety in the latter half of the 20th century and became renowned worldwide for its quality acts providing top entertainment. Fitting then for Tom Chaplin, singer of Keane, embarking on his first solo tour to take his place in the wings of this iconic venue. This was a top night- a celebration of life and music. Tom's solo album *'The Wave'* is a very personal record about his battle with addiction, much of which was showcased tonight. It was emotional and life giving, with that familiar tangible warmth[47] evident between performer and audience. He delivered his set (new album interspersed with Keane classics) with real gratitude and humility. At times his vocals touched the spirit with their purity and clarity. I went with Kirsten and somehow it did our souls good to be there.

---

[47] **See chapter 52**

Chapter 67 – Rock, Rick and Roll
Foo Fighters
O2 London 2017

What can you say about Dave Grohl and his band the Foo Fighters? Passionate, uncompromising, funny, crude, and totally lovable. Two things you have to be prepared for at a FF gig – constant use of the 'F' word, and non-stop full on rock for close on three hours.

Dom and I were towards the back of the arena for this one-off show to celebrate the release of the Foo's ninth studio album, *'Concrete and Gold'*. Some new songs were aired but this was largely a career-spanning set with a barrage of classic FF's tunes, one after another: *'My Hero', 'All My Life', 'The Pretender', 'Times like These', 'Walk', etc*, with Grohl occasionally pausing briefly for some outrageous comment. In one instance he picks out an embarrassed audience member heading toward the exit to ask him if he was going for a piss!

The set also included, the obligatory 'Queen' [48] cover - tonight's offering being *'Tie your Mother Down'*. But the surprise of the evening was Rick Astley on stage to perform his legendary pop anthem *'Never Gonna Give you up'*, but in a hard rock FF style. An extraordinary, bizarre moment! *'How am I supposed to follow that?"* asks Dave Grohl, who seemed as shocked as we were

---

[48] 'Queen' were the late drummer, Taylor Hawkins' favourite band

that this had actually just happened. But he does follow it by launching into a ten-minute version of '*Best of You*', half of which was the O2 singing the refrain repeatedly, refusing to stop even when the song finished.

This was a rock n' roll show at its finest.

Chapter 68 – One Tonight
Marillion (post Fish)
London Palladium 2017

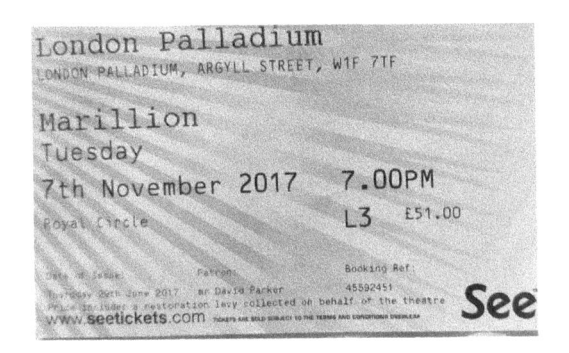

As I stated in Chapter 58, when Fish and Marillion parted company, I followed the former and ignored the latter. Over the last couple of years however, I had started to listen to some 'post Fish' Marillion with current vocalist Steve Hogarth. And there was plenty of choice to get my ears into – fifteen albums in fact. So, when they announced a show at the prestigious London Palladium, I went along. I got the very back seat in the circle, but this was no Wembley Arena, the great theatre had been designed to exclude no-one. The venue suited the band and I really enjoyed the two and a half hour set, which included the majority of the new album *'F.E.A.R.'* along with a few old gems thrown in from the Fish era including *'Heart of Lothian'* and *'Garden Party'*. The highlight though was the closing song – from the new album – the fifth part of 'The Leavers' entitled *'One Tonight'*. Singalongaheaven with stunning guitar solo and confetti sprayed high into the rafters of this historic theatre. It's what we want. Beautiful stuff!

Chapter 69 – Up Close and Personal
HMV Promo & Signings
HMV London 2017/2018

Throughout the year, HMV do regular promotion and signing events under the banner 'HMV Live'. Tickets are free but are essential. The entrance fee is the purchase of the artist's new album which you are obligated to buy. However, the artist does a live mini-set, after which there is a signing session. I managed to attend two of these, both at HMV on Oxford Street.

TOM CHAPLIN 2017
Six months to the day that I had seen Tom at the Palladium, it was now time for something completely different!

A great atmosphere as we walked down Oxford St to the HMV store. The Christmas lights were on, which was very appropriate as Tom was releasing his new Christmas album. On arrival at HMV and after serious queuing, we were led up several flights of stairs and through a maze of corridors to get to the top floor. He performed on a tiny stage with a full band. Most songs were off the new album, the highlight being *'Midnight Mass'*. There was a nice moment when he performed *'Somewhere Only We Know'* introducing it as a Lily Allen cover. I got the new album signed after further long queuing.

FRANK TURNER 2018 (Show 2169)

Ditto regarding everything above except the artist. FT was promoting *'Be more Kind'* and performed acoustically five or six new songs and a couple of oldies, *'Ballad of me and my Friends'* and *'Get Better'*. Fantastic to meet and greet.

Chapter 70 - An Anthemic Masterclass
Embrace
Shepherd's Bush Empire, London 2018

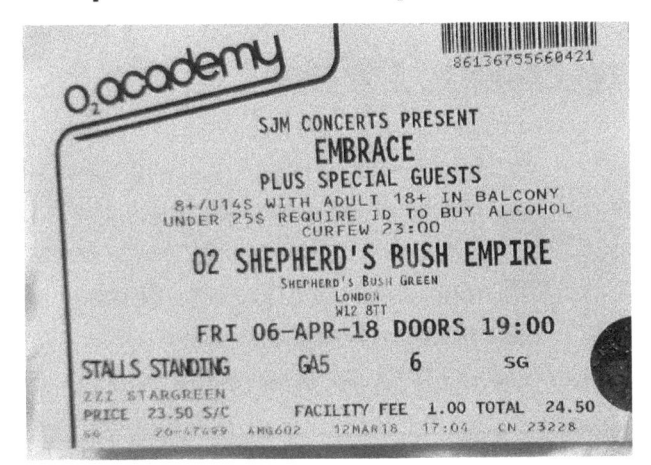

A Yorkshire band who have a huge following but have never quite made it to mega status. Formed in 1990, They have a host of great songs which have built up over three decades. On this night, we were treated to a master-class in anthemic pop-rock. Even if you didn't know the material, the band ensured you were able to participate, and everyone did. What impressed me was the incredible vibe. It was one of the best sustained crowd atmospheres of any gig. It was unrelenting. A fantastic night with great songs. I was also reminded that 'The Good will Out' is one of the best closing singalong songs of any band.

Chapter 71 – The Show Must Go On
Queen (post Freddie Gigs)
2008 – 2018

<u>With Paul Rogers - O2 2008</u>

An emotional night! 22 years after the infamous Wembley show, here I am, back in London to see 'Queen' tour with Paul Rogers, formally of 'Free' and 'Bad Company'.

Brian May & Roger Taylor had spent the years following Freddie's death working on the musical *'We Will Rock You'* and now that it was successfully underway, they were back focusing on a tour. I confess I was nervous. Queen without Freddie? How could it work? A joint album release prior to the tour *'The Cosmos Rocks'* didn't inspire confidence. It came across as very ordinary and mediocre, even bland. Would the gig follow suit, in which case it could be a disaster?

Well, the answer thankfully was 'No'! The one key stipulation on being able to enjoy this concert was to reconcile the fact that Paul wasn't Freddie and could never try to be. Once you accepted that, you could enjoy the show for what it was. The vast majority of the set was classic Queen songs which worked quite well with Paul's voice, and there were a few contributions from his back catalogue, notably a fantastic version of the Free song *'All Right Now'*. The inescapable factor though, that lifted the show was of course Brian's guitar style, ensuring the sound of Queen was there in its perfect best, and that somehow ensured the spirit of Queen inhabited the show.

The most memorable moment was in *'Love of My Life'*, a song which live was always performed as a duet with Freddie and Brian. Tonight, Brian brought on stage an empty stool and 20,000 voices sang Freddie's lyrics of the song in his absence. Profoundly moving.

In 2009, after five years, Paul Rodgers announced he was parting ways with Queen stating *"It was never a permanent arrangement"*. Roger Taylor, when asked simply said *"He was his own Man"*.

With Adam Lambert – Hammersmith Apollo 2012

Rumours were rife as to who may become the new Queen singer. Names bandied around included Gary Cherone (of Extreme) and George Michael, both because of their contributions at the Freddie tribute concert. Tom Chaplin also attracted speculation after an amazing performance with Queen at a Prince's Trust Concert in 2010. But the answer came in the form of a young, flamboyant singer called Adam Lambert. Queen and Lambert first performed together in 2009 when Brian May and Roger Taylor appeared as guests on the eighth season of *American Idol* in which Lambert was a contestant. He came runner up in the competition, but something clicked and in 2012, six shows were confirmed around Europe billed as 'Queen and Adam Lambert'. I was at one of the three London shows at the Hammersmith Apollo (former Odeon). I had standing tickets so for the first time since the Ally Pally gig in 1979, I was near the front at a Queen Concert. It was a great night. Of course, Lambert was on trial big time. For me, it took a bit of getting used to, but he did great and I was won over as much as was possible. His voice was stunning and I really liked his approach when he confessed that he wasn't trying to be Freddie or even replace him, but he was there to celebrate him along with us. Two memorable aspects of this show: one was that Brian had a camera attached to his guitar so we got close ups on screen of his virtuoso solos and riffs. The other was a shared Bo Rhap vocal between Lambert and Freddie on screen. Tears ahoy!

With Adam Lambert - Wembley Arena 2018

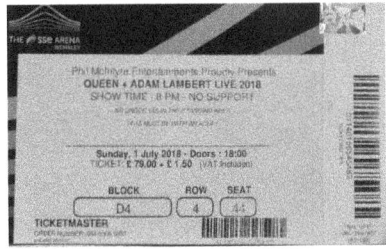

The same quartet of us that were at the 1986 gig, were back at Wembley 32 years on for a spectacular show in typical Queen tradition.

It was 40 years since the album, *'News of the World'* was released, with its iconic sci-fi themed front cover, depicting a robot decimating the four band members. In recognition, the robot became the centre of this tour's stage show, a gigantic, mechanical autotron, extending to the heights of the arena roof. He makes his initial introduction by breaking through a wall and peering out over the audience, creating a slight feeling of unease (especially if you are aware of the inner gatefold artwork of the NOTW album). He then continues to pop-up through the show, once when his giant head appears through the floor with Adam Lambert draped over, and once to bear Brian May high up performing a classic solo. The lighting show was something else too – multi coloured lasers, dramatic silhouettes, themed backdrops and superb animations using the *'Kind of Magic'* cartoon figures. There's a moment of wonder when Freddie makes an appearance in *'Love of My Life'* [See Appendix A:5] plus a stunning *'Who wants to live Forever'*, dramatic in its laser spotlighting and stunning vocals.

As for Lambert, he is of course no longer on trial. Everyone knows what to expect and that has enabled him to somewhat develop his own identity within Queen. It seems to me he cleverly uses his own exuberant persona as a camp showman, which replicates Freddie, yet doesn't take anything from him. So, for example at the end, when he appears in crown and gold cape, it never seems like he is trying to steal Freddie's iconic Wembley '86 image, rather it comes across as a neat tribute.

Of course, a Queen show will always leave a hole. Freddie is gone and will never be replaced. But the determination of Brian & Roger that the show must go on, and to keep the spirit, sound and songs of Queen alive, is admirable and important beyond measure.

Chapter 72 – A Family Affair
Biffy Clyro
Royal Albert Hall, London 2018

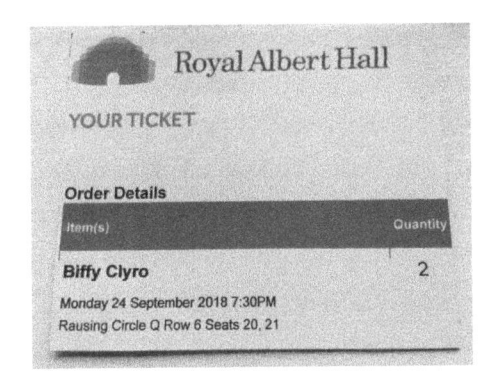

A classy venue for the highly esteemed Scottish rock band, one of Dom's favourite bands and one I'd come to appreciate. This was an acoustic tour and it was great to hear the songs reworked from the familiar heavier full on band versions. Two significant things I picked up from this evening.

First is that Biffy exude as much power acoustically than most bands do electronically, and virtually all the songs transition brilliantly. Tonight, for example *'Biblical'*, *'Black Chandelier'*, *'Many of Horror'*, *'Mountains'*, and especially *'Bubbles'* (c/f Appendix A:6). They came across, albeit with less noise, but with equal muscle, intensity and potency, helped along with the audience accompaniment. This brings me to the second thing, and that is the fans. Unlike any other band I've come across, the Biffy Clyro 'family' (and I use that word deliberately because that what it feels like) have a culture of their own. Not only do they know all the lyrics but there is a rapport, a 'language' almost, that is unique. I felt on the edge of this, knowing enough to understand it existed but not knowing enough to be able to readily enter in. The great thing is it didn't stop me from being able to belt out the songs, and have a great time. I left the gig feeling this was a band I wanted to stay in touch with, not only because of the great songs but because of the unique package they provided. Maybe the next step should be the full-on electric gig.

Chapter 73 – Brothers in Arms
Mark Knopfler
O2 London 2019

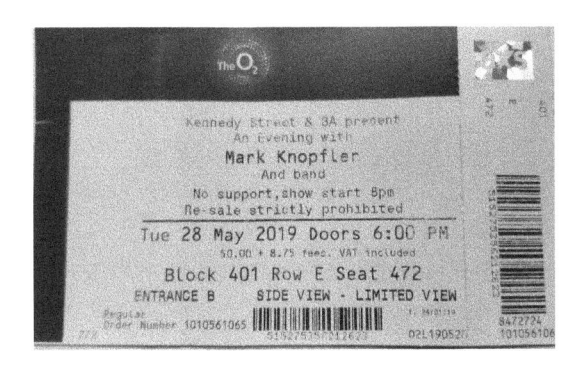

What a joy to be able to turn back the clock and taste once again the live music of Mark Knopfler and Dire Straits. When DS finally called it a day in 1988, Mark went solo. He must have wondered how that would all turn out? Well, here he was forty years on, now aged seventy, at one of several sold-out shows at the O2. So, I guess the answer is, it turned out OK, and soaking in the warmth and togetherness of the crowd, could there have been any real doubts?

This was a wonderful evening with the best sound quality of any gig I can remember. Knopfler himself seemed physically sluggish and moved very slowly, but his guitar work was far from it. Still with his unmistakable finger picking technique, and a top-quality backing band, he conjured up some magic with a blend of solo material and old DS songs, including *'Romeo & Juliet'* and *'Brothers in Arms'*, beautifully re-worked with a blend of sax, flute and piano. He finished the set (as he did when I last saw him in 1985) with *'Going Home'* the instrumental from the film *'Local Hero'.* Trouble is, I didn't want to. I could honestly have sat through the show again!

Knopfler – Still Finger Pickin' Good

PART SIX
THE 2020s

Chapter 74 – From Cake Tins to Concert Halls
Calva Louise
The Roundhouse London 2020

Nerves were edgy as I stood waiting for Calva Louise to take the stage. Next to me were Kirsten & Dom waiting in anticipation. Three years after an opening slot at the *'Roundhouse Rising'* Festival, they were back - this time to headline! This just seemed to be one of those milestone nights for the band, that tend to crop up in between the months and years of hard work, writing, recording and touring.

The lights go down and the band take the stage to a bit of dry ice. Jess Allanic on guitar and vocals, Alizon Taho on bass guitar and Ben Parker on drums... who also I should add, is my son. So, allow me to pause and reflect just for a moment.

The first thing to say is I'm never surprised to see Ben onstage behind the drums - it has always been a natural passion. From as early as two years old, he was organising cake tins around him on the floor and beating the living daylights out of them with a pair of six inch green plastic toy drumsticks. For his third birthday we bought an old cheap drum kit which we set up in the lounge the night before his birthday. When he came down on birthday morning, he climbed on it and started to drum an in-time rhythm. It's always been 'in him', and he's always loved to play. Over the years we've been to a fair few gigs to see him drum, both with former band, Pistol Kings as well as current band, Calva Louise. A few shows along the way that stand out in my memory are:

2015 – LECHLADE FESTIVAL – The First 'festival' gig Pistol Kings had was at Walthamstow the previous year, and involved playing to a crowd of six people, four of whom were parents including us. Here at Lechlade in the Cotswolds, the band fared much better. Headliners on the main stage were Status Quo. Although the boys played on a smaller stage, they still got a fair crowd and some fans wanting photos afterwards.

2015 – EP LAUNCH at the Garage. A wild night in a sweaty upper room. Heaps of fun. The single off the EP *Run Roger* (which I still love) went off at the end of the set.

2016 – PUNK WEEKENDER at the Roundhouse. The first time I'd seen the trio play under the name of 'Mystified'. Ben had been asked to help out for some gigs due to a departing drummer. Something clicked and Ben made the tough choice to leave Pistol Kings and become the permanent replacement for Mystified. Here they pulled it off at the Roundhouse with an undeniable chemistry, a strong presence and catchy punk-pop songs. A couple of months later, I saw them rebranded as 'Calva Louise' at the venue 229.

2016 – WYCHWOOD FESTIVAL in Gloucestershire. Good score on the main stage, but being the first act on around midday, meant the crowds hadn't yet gathered and the band seemed a bit lost on the huge platform, under the bright sun. Still, it was a great day. We as a family landed backstage passes, and it was good to see the band enjoying hospitality and having their own dressing room (which just so happened to be next to Bill Bailey, the comedian.)

2018 – SUPPORTING SPRING KING at the Waterfront Norwich. The band's first real tour, and a show on home turf. Impacted by the crowd singing along to lyrics of their songs, especially *'Getting Closer'*. Had to remind myself that this is what is supposed to happen!

2018 – SUPPORTING HUNTER & THE BEAR at The Scala London. Brilliant venue holding about 800. CL were pushing their debut album *'Rhinoceros'* and played most of this. HATB were brilliant. Grunty melodic singalong rock with *'Hologram'* and *'Paper Heart'* standing out.

2019 – SUPPORTING THE MAINE at the Forum, Kentish Town, London. 2,300 capacity sold out. I was in the circle and had a perspective of a bigger 'CL'. Jess starting to awaken to the rock star she is, with good crowd rapport and the band handled the bigger stage well. A great moment after CL's set during the equipment changeover when the Killers *'Mr Brightside'* came on over the sound system and the crowd picked up on it. It seemed to spread like wildfire and by midway through, the whole audience were singing every word.

2020 – HEADLINING ROUNDHOUSE RISING at the Roundhouse... and so back to the gig with which I started the chapter.

The band took a few songs to warm up and settle nerves but they powered through their set mixing some 'Rhinoceros' tracks (*'Outrageous'/ 'Wondertale' / 'I'm Gonna do well'*) with newer material – the rousing *'Belicoso'* off 2019's EP *'Interlude for the Borderline'* and the outstanding *'Camino'* off 2020's EP *'Popurri'*, which sees the band experimenting with different electronic sounds. It was a milestone night.

Since this gig in 2020, the band have gone from strength to strength. Surviving lockdown, they emerged the other side of the pandemic with a second Album *'Euphoric'*, and more recently, some newer songs with heavier sounds moving more towards the 'metal' genre. Probably not my style of choice, but one that seems to have done no harm at all. An extensive twenty five date tour of the USA supporting 'Slothrust' happened in 2022 with further UK, US and European tours/ festivals in 2023/24 including Download at Donington and Riotfest in Chicago. 2025 sees the band playing 'ShipRocked', a metal festival held on a cruise ship visiting the Bahamas and Virgin Islands. [Don't suppose there's a guest pass for this one?]

It goes without saying I love to see the band play live and I love to see Ben drum live. From the cake tin days to now, I've seen his journey slowly unfold and the dedication, practice, and the 10,000 hours he's put in. [49]

There's obviously the 'proud Dad' aspect to all this but I've also come to realise after all these years that when I do see him play, I know now that I'm watching a very, very good drummer.

---

[49] **A much-touted theory originally aired by Malcolm Gladwell in his book *'Outliers'* which suggests if you want to get really proficient at something or achieve a level of expertise, you need to practise the skill for 10,000 hours.**

Chapter 75 – Thankful
The Calling
B2 venue Norwich 2020

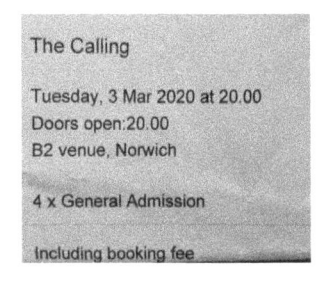

> The Calling
>
> Tuesday, 3 Mar 2020 at 20.00
> Doors open:20.00
> B2 venue, Norwich
>
> 4 x General Admission
>
> Including booking fee

A band I'd never thought I'd see. I have loved the Calling ever since the release of the album 'Camino Palmero' back in 2002 and the single from it, 'Wherever You May Go' which is one of my all-time favorite songs. But after releasing a second album, the band split up. Vocalist, Alex Band, pursued a solo career on and off for the next twenty years but finally they reformed, and here they were in Norwich in a small intimate venue.

Some bands that I hear, as good as the songs may be, sound dated. Not the Calling – the sound seems as fresh today as twenty years ago when they first were aired, and Alex's voice as distinctive and powerful as ever. One song that stood out to me tonight was 'Thank you' – a song full of spiritual overtone. I found during the set I had a strong feeling of thankfulness for some reason or another. I think it was just having the opportunity to see this band and enjoy a night with friends. On the way home though, I commented to my gig going pal how much energy Alex seemed to have. "Yes, it's amazing" he replied, Especially as he has 'Parkinson's Disease.'

WHAT!?

Alex Band has Parkinsons?

I never knew! I wanted to turn back and try and see him, to encourage and thank him. He had masked it so well on stage, and believe you me, that was something I knew all about. I was an expert myself in masking. Again, the sense of gratitude welled up – both from the fact that he'd had the strength to perform and I'd had the strength to be there and enjoy.

Little did I know this show was one of the last few gigs in the whole country because in a few days time, we would be in COVID lockdown, and everything would cease to be.

Covid Confessions

I confess it all seems like a dream now. Life is back to normal, and the world of lock downs, isolation and no gigs seems a distant memory.

However, whilst the circus is over, the repercussions are still very much with us. This is especially true for the music industry, one of the areas that has been hit hardest by the pandemic. Cancelations of live performances and tours was only half the picture. Artists also cancelled album releases because they had no tour to promote them. This effectively brought performance revenue down to zero. However, this devastating sudden loss of income affected not just the artists but the significant related industries that work in and alongside them – promoters, road crew, transport companies, security guards, and of course the venues and all the staff they employ. Sadly, several venues ended up closing.

Artists also fighting to survive began to seek new ways to both engage with their fan base, and to attempt to create some kind of income. In 2020, there was a new movement in online performance. Services like Twitch evolved providing a streaming platform enabling artists to go direct from their own home or studio to their fanbase. So both small-time performers and established stars like Chris Martin and John Legend delivered gigs from Living Rooms!

It was a time for new ideas, and those creatively minded who were prepared to go out on a limb were often rewarded. Ben Folds, the US rock musician was touring in Australia when the pandemic forced him to prematurely cancel his concerts.

Lockdowned in Sydney, Folds began to host four live streams a week, performing concerts for his fans. But he went one step further – for a monthly charge of $10, fans got exclusive access to archive footage, piano classes, songwriting tutorials, and question and answer sessions. This initiative enabled him to earn enough to cover his entire rent in Sydney. Another example of creativity in adversity is Mike Peters and the Alarm Staycations (see next chapter 76).

Of course, there should also be a mention to all regular gig-goers. They too suffered in these times of isolation. During the lockdown, many messages were coming from scientists and psychologists warning that the cost of isolation may outweigh the benefits, with concerns of a loneliness crisis, creation of a fear culture and a huge rise in clinical depression caused by a drop in a key chemical messenger that helps us feel good. Concerts and live events are one vehicle for this. Sadly, these messages in many cases didn't (or weren't allowed to) get through.

There's no doubt the pandemic was disastrous for the music world – the artists, the industry and the fans. But were there any positives out of all this? I think the answer is 'Yes'.

My first gig back after COVID was the 'Manics' at Cambridge. As I mentioned in Chapter 59, there were strong emotions flying about that night from both band and audience. We had all had a rude awakening in assuming gigs would always exist and happen, until suddenly they couldn't and didn't. The return to live shows brought a natural & overwhelming sense of gratitude, appreciation and thankfulness for the freedom and joy of gathering together to celebrate the gift of music, I for one, confess I have vowed never again to take for granted what is the wonder of the live gig.

Chapter 76 – An intimate weekend with a Rock Star
The Alarm Experience 40
Dyserth, Wales 2022

Being part of an intimate gig of only 17 people and contributing to the setlist played – that was the highlight of this very special event.

The Alarm have played a significant part in my musical journey. (c/f Chapter 39) Both Kirsten & I would call ourselves fans. However, we peter into insignificance compared to our dear friends and gig going companions who are massive followers. We have attended many Alarm gigs together, some of which have been documented in this book, but there are two events that certainly need a mention.

Way back in 1998 we attended an annual event *'The Gathering'* in Wales, which is a weekend where Alarm fans come together, and Mike Peters usually does an acoustic set on the Friday night and a full electric set on the Saturday. One memory that stands out from this time in Wales, was that it coincided with one of the warmest January weekends on record and we were walking along the sea front in t-shirts.

And then in 2022 we had the privilege of attending an Alarm staycation, which our friends bought us as a surprise gift for Christmas. So, in July of that year, we embarked on an adventure that proved to be very special.

Before a run-down of that, a brief word about Mike Peters, whose story is incredibly inspirational. In essence, he has been battling cancer for over 25 years. He has had three major 'attacks' in 1996, 2006 and 2022, plus his wife (and band keyboardist) Jules, has had her own battle with breast cancer. On every occasion they have risen up and defied the odds, showing a resilience that is truly remarkable. In the midst of all this, they set up the cancer charity: the *'Love Hope Strength'* Foundation[50]. Mike is often involved in playing fund raising gigs in unusual places – so far, these include at the top of Snowden, the Sahara, The Alps and Mount Everest base camp (with thirty eight other musicians)– the highest concert ever to have taken place.

Now back to the Staycation. This was an idea that came out of COVID lockdown when it was impossible to tour. Mike & Jules' philosophy was if you couldn't go to fans why not get the fans to come to you. So as soon as restrictions relaxed, the weekend staycations began They were held in the village of Dyserth, an area of outstanding beauty, which also happens to be M & J's home village. Here is a run-down of the weekend.

THURSDAY - The accommodation was in the former Bethel Chapel right opposite the waterfall in the heart of the village. There were five units all with 'Alarm' themed names – we were in the *'Strength'* apartment, which had memorabilia dotted around. Once

---

[50] Go to *lovehopestrength.co.uk* to be inspired and to donate

we had settled in, we gathered in the lobby and Mike and Jules arrived and welcomed us, and then we enjoyed a champagne reception in the beautiful gardens at the rear of the chapel, where we conversed with our hosts and fellow guests.

FRIDAY – In the evening, we took a short walk to the venue where the *'Big Night In'* was produced and broadcast. The *'Big Night in'* was again birthed out of the pandemic. It was a live streamed broadcast hosted by Mike and Jules which each week comprised of discussion and live music from Mike, old footage, videos and stories behind the songs and past tours. Since COVID restrictions had relaxed, we the 'Staycationers' were the live audience. It was a great and different night being part of the recording that was being streamed around the globe, and watching the production and organisation behind it all. Naturally beverages were available including a couple of crafted beers. I tried the *'Drunk and Disorderly'* whilst K went for the *'Sound and the Fury'*. Our friends ended up being interviewed by Mike & Jules as part of the broadcast, which produced a smile from them that didn't disappear the whole weekend.

SATURDAY – We spent a cold day at the beach, exploring the coast and townships, but all focus was on the highlight of the weekend, our own unique private gig where we could request songs for the setlist. This of course meant no two shows were ever the same. Figuring he would play all the faves anyway, I chose two lesser well known songs: *'Train a Comin'* off Mike's first solo album *'Breathe'* and *'Raindown'* off *'Under Attack'*, which I've always found a powerful song spiritually. It was a special night, 17 Staycationers being entertained by a rock legend. And at the end we were up and singing as if there was 17,000 of us, and when eventually the *'Going out in a Blaze of Glory'* refrain faded, we took the short walk back to our apartment, knowing we'd partaken in a very special experience.

SUNDAY – For the last morning we met Mike and Jules in the park opposite the chapel and had some final photos in front of the waterfall. Mike did a signing session before we bid farewell, and we headed back on the long drive to Norfolk., taking with us some amazing memories. In the words of an Alarm song:

*'These moments in time,
live on forever in my mind.'* [51]

Mike compiles our Setlist

---

[51] **'Moments in Time' off the Alarm's 'Raw' album**

Chapter 77 – So Happy it Hurts
Bryan Adams
Royal Albert Hall London 2022/ NEC Birmingham 1987

I saw Bryan Adams back in 1987 at the NEC. It was a tour to promote his fifth studio album *'Into the Fire'*. The album had a lot to live up to following 1984's brilliant *'Reckless'*. And to be honest, it didn't! It was a bit of a disappointment in comparison. The gig at the NEC was great though. I remember T'Pau supporting. They were at their peak of their popularity having hit the No 1 spot with *'China in your hand'*, and brought it home. What I remember about Bryan Adams was the false starts of *'Summer of 69'*. Played as an encore, he started with the song's instantly recognisable riff, but instead of launching into *'I got my first real six-string'*, he teasingly launched into different classic summer songs (e.g. Mungo Jerry's *'In the Summertime'*/ Don Henley's *'The Boys of Summer'*). When it was actually time for the real thing, all he needed was to sing *'I Got...'* and the NEC took over the rest. It was such a good version of the song, that two subsequent encores seemed too much.

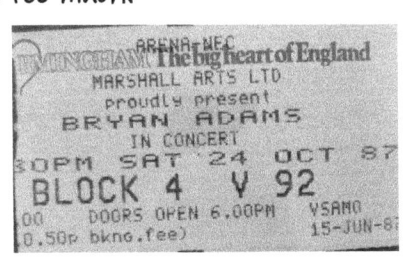

On to the Royal Albert Hall. This was a twice delayed gig due to the COVID pandemic, so it took place two years later than the original intended date. The first thing to mention is that on entry to the auditorium, there was a flying car [yes, I said flying car]. I know this venue is steeped in history and has seen so much, but I'm sure it's the first time it has had a giant inflatable full sized Chevrolet Corsair Convertible soaring around the domed rafters and over the audience.

Was this a new strategy developed during COVID to relieve waiting time pre gig? Whilst it certainly achieved this goal, the car was in fact a connection to B.A.'s fifteenth studio album 'So Happy it Hurts' featuring on the cover and in the video for the title track single release.

The drones brought the car safely into land just prior to the band taking the stage, and we were then treated to a vintage rock gig. I think it was pretty much the same band line up that played in '87. They knew each other inside out and the result was a highly polished, professional show. We had great seats in the choir stalls, which had a slightly rear view of the stage, but very close. Appropriately, I can vouch that 'the choir' was in full voice as we got a full run through of 'Into the Fire' before an interval and a substantial greatest hits second half, which included 'Run to You', 'Heaven', 'Can't Stop this Thing we Started' and 'Everything I Do', the latter dedicated to George

Michael. We left with sore throats and happy hearts –
So Happy it Hurts... very appropriate!

Oh yes ...and we also bumped into Stuart Pierce, the former English footballing hard man in the bar at half time! Score!

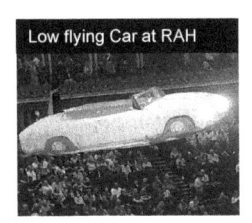

Chapter 78 - Love is Here
Starsailor
Waterfront Norwich 2022

Starsailor are a band I have really enjoyed over several years. When I saw this gig advertised, I briefly entertained getting tickets but the one person I knew who was familiar with this band, wasn't available as a gig companion, so I laid the idea to rest. However, two weeks before the gig, my son, Ben, texted me to say that his former band mate in Pistol Kings, Tom, was supporting SS with his new band 'The Howlers'. Some brief online communication later, and I was on the guest list.

The Howlers did well as a support – some promising signs for the future. Starsailor, on the other hand, have plenty of years behind them. They are often placed alongside bands like Coldplay, Turin Brakes and Travis[52] as pioneers of the 'New Acoustic Movement' around the turn of the century. This tour was a twentieth anniversary celebration of *'Love is Here'*, their debut album from 2001. Frontman James Walsh has a unique

James Walsh - Raw Emotion

---

[52] **Travis guitarist, Andy Dunlop, played bass at this gig, filling in for normal SS bassist James Stelfox, while he, as James Walsh put it, *'was doing his thing'*. I later found out this *'thing'* he was doing was touring with another band in Europe!**

voice, distinctive and powerful, and this was accentuated live. The ability to belt one song out with sheer raw power, and follow it up with another filled with such tender, heartfelt emotion was an experience to behold. In return the warmth of response from the crowd was tangible.

Appendage on this gig: Tom asked if 'The Howlers' could crash overnight at ours. On return from the gig, we waited up for them. However, they got held up so we ended up giving them directions and leaving the back door open. We found out next morning they had difficulty finding our house in the dark. Even when they came in though the back door, they still weren't entirely sure it was the right place. Apparently, they crept around for some time trying to find evidence of something to confirm they were in the right place. Eventually they saw a 'Calva Louise' album by the record player and breathed a huge sigh of relief. Couldn't help but snigger at the thought of the band creeping around someone else's house and having to explain that one to the police.

Chapter 79: Glory Day
Bruce Springsteen
Hyde Park, London 2023

You wouldn't have thought I would be starting with a negative, but I am. But it's not really the gig, it's the tickets - or lack of them. Not for the first time, entry is electronically, via a QR code, but for the first time this is literally just a barcode: no ticket. Permission to mourn for the loss of something integral to gig going!

Now that's over, let's get real! This was a joyous, celebratory concert by one of the world's true iconic legends. One of the few artists I have wanted to see live finally becomes a reality, and it even surpassed my high expectations.

But where to start?

In the opening words of the first song from my old pal, Frank Turner: *'Let's begin at the beginning'* [53] Frank was one of two main supports on the main stage and poured high energy into a great forty minute set. Ignoring the other main billed support, US country pop

---

[53] **The opening line to the song '*I knew Prufrock before he got famous*'**

band 'The Chicks', we wandered over to the Rainbow stage to see Irish Rock Band 'The Coronas'. There was virtually no one there when they started, but the audience gradually built. They were fantastic with a charismatic front man in singer and pianist, Danny O Reilly. He spent the whole of one song mixing with the crowd going from person to person, hugging, hi-fiving and shaking hands. An immensely likable band.

Back to the main stage for the Boss!

What to say? First up, Bruce Springsteen is now seventy-three years old. He performed for just over three hours without any sign of his energy levels dipping. Whilst the rest of the band enjoyed a couple of breaks during the set, Bruce never left the stage once. His voice sounded as good as ever with the gravelly low notes complimenting and contrasting the almost angelic high ones.

Of course, a good portion of the success of Bruce is the E- Street band. They have now been together for fifty years and are understandably a super-tight outfit, knowing each other inside out - the result is a totally professional show of the highest quality. But what is clear is that the relationship between them all is so very obviously genuine – they undeniably love doing what they do. And it's quite right that Steve van Zandt, the guitarist dressed in the pirate outfit, Nils Lofgren, the guitarist dressed like a cowboy, as well as pianist, Roy Bitten and drummer, Max Weinberg are legends in their own rights. It seems obvious to me that when Bruce does his three hours, it's not because that's what's expected, but because clearly, he loves the songs he plays and who he's playing them with.

And so, 7pm on a warm summer's evening, the band take to the stage one by one, Bruce being the last to appear amidst the now familiar personal chant of the crowd "Bruuuuccee." And we're away… with the band power-launching into 'No Surrender'.

<u>The First Hour</u> – The show kicks off at a frantic pace. We are pummelled by a non-stop series of rockers – 'Prove it all Night', 'Promised Land' and 'Out in the Street', feature early. There is no pause for breath here, just the 1-2-3-4 count to bridge the last song into the next. It's relentless!

<u>The Second Hour</u> - The pace does slacken eventually mid concert, but there's a price to pay. The body gets a respite in 'My Hometown' but the vocal cords are called to step up a gear with Bruce leading a massive congregational singalong. Then we're treated to 'The River' - a beautiful song, tenderly performed with some harmonica complimenting the piano background. But before we know it, we're back to some upbeat songs with a brilliant version of the Commodore's 'Nightshift'. All through, Bruce is clearly having fun, often making the journey from the main stage down the steps to audience level, where he shakes some hands, wears some hats, poses for some selfies, and hands out guitar picks and harmonicas to a lucky few. He rarely engages in actual banter with the audience, presumably preferring

to let the music do the talking. The one exception though, (and the highlight of the second hour for me) was a song called *'Last Man Standing'*, where Bruce shared the story of his very first band and the fact that he is now the only surviving member. There was a hush that descended on the crowd in what was a truly sobering and emotional moment.

<u>The Third Hour</u> – Classics all the way from this point on. *'The Rising'* merges into *'Badlands'* and then the closer *'Thunder Road'* with a stunning sax and brass accompaniment to the instrumental ending.

"They think it's all over...?" Not a chance! The encore is to come which, let's face it, is the length of most bands' complete set. Bruce tells us he's just warming up as we're launched into another onslaught of iconic classics – *Born in the USA, Born to Run, Bobby Jean, Glory Days* and *Dancing in the Dark,* all follow one another in a pure celebratory atmosphere. Finally, the band leave the stage and Bruce is left alone with his acoustic guitar for a touching final song, *'I'll see you in my Dreams',* a song that causes us to contemplate our own mortality and one that unexpectedly leaves a tinge of sadness in the air, as Bruce leaves for the last time.

But I can't leave this gig report on a note of sadness, because to be honest it was a party through and through. So back to my highlight of the third hour – *'Glory Days'.*

Back in 2012 when Bruce played Hyde Park, there was a famous incident where he overran curfew and the promoters pulled the plug mid song, causing an uproar.

Tonight, he re-visited the incident in an hilarious jibe. Half way through a blistering version of *'Glory Days',* he suddenly stops dead and says to guitarist Steve, *'Stevie, I think it's time to go home?'* Over loud booing, Steve responds as the voice and complaint of the crowd *'say what?*

Bruce repeats, 'No honestly Stevie, I think it's time to go home!' Louder Booing!

Steve repeats his questioning *'Say WHAT?'*

Bruce: *'I'm telling you, they are going to pull the f***** plug again...'* A massive cheer...Bruce says something like *'Oh what the hell'* and to the joy and laughter of 70,000 people, they re-launch back into Glory Days.

Laughter, tears, joy, celebration, dancing, oneness, and very good music! This truly was a Glory Day!

Chapter 80: Back to Beginnings
The Sweet
Waterfront Norwich 2022

Andy Scott – one foot in the grave?

At the start of this book, I shared that the first band to influence me were glam rock pioneers, *The Sweet*.

I had seen The Sweet twice before live. Once in 1981 at Queen Mary's College, London where the original band members minus vocalist Brian Connolly, played a riotous gig. Then 10 years later I saw Brian Connolly's Sweet which was Brian with a new band. Sadly, due to ill health, he was a shadow of his old self and the best part of that gig were fellow glam rockers 'Mud' led by original vocalist Les Gray.[54]

Now twenty years later on from that, and fifty years since my beginnings when *'Blockbuster'* first hit the airwaves, I was back for more - on what turned out to be a freezing cold December night.

This time, the band had the only surviving member of the original four still going – guitarist Andy Scott, aged seventy three years old. And give the dude his due,

---

[54] **Who could forget 'Tiger Feet', one of the glam greats.**

in between jokingly complaining of arthritis, a trapped nerve and incontinence, he could still deliver some mean riffs and solos. And he was loving it, as were all of us in the packed crowd. We danced, moshed and sung every word of the classic Sweet hits: 'Fox on the Run', 'Love is like Oxygen', 'Teenage Rampage', 'Hellraiser', etc plus 'Ballroom Blitz' alongside 'Blockbuster' as encores. Fifty Years somehow rolled away and I was back at the beginning again.

One great moment was after a long spiel from Andy about how committed he was to continuing touring and playing, an audience member shouted out from the front, "So will you be back here next year?" To which Andy, after a brief pause, retorted: "*If I'm still alive – definitely!*".

One day at a time, I guess - which leads me to a few final closing confessions...

Epilogue
Closing Confessions

The sun rises and the sun sets, then hurries back to where it rises. The wind blows to the south, and then turns to the north, round and round it goes, ever returning on its course. All streams flow into the sea, yet the sea is never full. To the place streams come from, there they return again... What has been will be again, what has been done will be done again, there is nothing new under the sun.

Ecclesiastes 1:6-9 (New International Version)

I confess that I find 'time' a mysterious thing. When I was younger, I remember hearing over and over again from older generations, that the more you advance in years, the quicker time passes. Now I am one of the older generations, I can testify that 'yes', it really does seem to. And as the weeks blend into months and the months into years, I find myself increasingly contemplating the thoughts *"Where has the time gone?"* and *'where did the years go?* It is somewhat comforting that in the ancient 3,000 year old writings above, the author of Ecclesiastes, wrestled with similar issues and thoughts. Maybe this is where we gleaned the modern day saying, *'What goes around comes around'.* Certainly, for me, The Sweet gig epitomised this truth for me. It was a moment when *"the streams"* of fifty years of gigs, which I have fondly revisited in this book, came back to the start, a complete circle returning to the point of beginning. Of course, I haven't finished yet and whilst I doubt whether *'Confessions Volume 2... the next fifty years'* will ever be written, (I'll have one hundred and thirteen candles on my cake by then), I will continue to attend gigs as I'm able.

I have a great t-shirt that has a 'rock gig' style design and the wording: *"Still Rockin' after all these years"*. However, the main graphic, which you would expect to be a guitar or similar rock n' roll image, is in fact a rocking chair! I tend to wear this when I go to a gig. The reason being is it acts as a personal reminder/statement to myself not to shrink back into a safe little world that's easy and familiar. Without doubt life, including gig-going, gets more challenging as the days tick by, but I want to take each day more and more for what it is – a gift – and live it well and full and be in the now. None of us can change yesterday nor can we predict tomorrow. All we have is today – this moment right now - and all we can do is to be present today. It's just like Andy Scott's response from the last chapter: *'If I'm alive I'll be there'.*

One final thought: pop and rock music will shortly enter a new age. Right now, as I write there is a generation still alive that were living in the mid 1950s when rock n' roll was born. But in the not-too-distant future, a time will come when that will no longer be the case. Then a decade after that, there will be no one that witnessed 'Beatlemania' first hand. And then a decade after that, no one alive from my musical generation who wore bell bottoms & platform shoes and experienced the glam rock era. My point is *what will happen then?* Will bands from bygone ages fade away?

will the celebrated stars of each musical genre be forgotten? [55] The answer is of course, we don't know. However, whilst pondering my Top 3s for the Appendix, it hit me just how timeless great songs are. The truth is, I firmly believe people will still be singing the greats 50 years/ 100 years/ 200 years from now. Great songs are destined to outlive the singers that sung them and the bands that played them.

Ultimately though, that's a thing only the strange phenomena called 'time', will tell.

---

[55] We had a friend round for a coffee with 2 daughters in their early teens. During conversation, George Michael was mentioned. One of the girls said, 'Who is George Michael?' Neither of the daughters knew who he was!

Appendices

APPENDIX A
My Top 3s

APPENDIX B
Index of Bands/ Artists seen live

APPENDIX C
Acknowledgements

APPENDIX A
My Top 3...

1. All Time Gigs
2. Live Songs
3. Singalong Anthems
4. Special Moments
5. Powerful Moments
6. 'Take off' Moments
7. Best Starts
8. Vocalists
9. Drummers
10. Guitar solos
11. Disappointments
12. Bizarre and Funny Moments
13. Artists I wish I'd Seen
14. Photos with the Stars

1. TOP 3 All Time Gigs

1. Queen – Wembley Stadium 1986
For the reasons detailed in Chapter 33, I have no difficulty in choosing or hesitation in awarding the No.1 top spot in my personal history of gig-going, to this event. Simply the best.

2. Queen – Earl's Court 1977
Maybe because this was my first real gig. The experience and emotions involved were in a sense my birth into gig going. I can still recall vivid things from this concert.

3. Michael Jackson – Wembley 1988
For the sheer grandeur and brilliance of the event, and the components which made it way more than a music concert, but an experience on so many different levels.

2. TOP 3 Live Songs

1. In the Cage/ Cinema Show/ Afterglow Medley – Genesis

As referred to in Chapter 23, this medley was a permanent fixture within the Genesis live setlist. Yet it varied on every tour. It always started with the unorthodox *'In the Cage'* and always finished with the evocative *'Afterglow'*. Mostly it contained the awesome instrumental section of 'Cinema Show' and it always included Collins and Thompson together on drums. My favourite version is from the *'Live in Rome'* recording where *'Duke's Travels'* features, leading into *'Afterglow'*. An absolutely stunning piece of music, that I can just drink in and get lost within its wide expansive boundaries.

2. A Design for Life – Manic Street Preachers

A firm favourite at any Manics live gig, and undoubtedly a special song. *'Libraries gave us Power'* is the iconic opening lyric which launches into what is, simply an epic, politically charged song. I waited a long time to hear it played live, just knowing how good it was going to be. I wasn't disappointed. My only issue with this song is that it is too short.

3. 23 – Jimmy Eat World

Again, eagerly anticipated, and turned out to be even better live than the recorded version.

3. TOP 3 Singalong Anthems

This differs from the previous category in that they are perhaps not such high-quality songs in themselves, but they were written to sing along to. An anthem is something that everyone knows, and is very much part of the one-ness that is a highlight of a successful gig.

Choosing a Top 3 is incredibly difficult, but I have to put in at the top:

1. We Will Rock You/ We are The Champions – Queen

Released as a double A sided single in 1977 and from that time on, always formed part of the encore to the live set, concluding the show in unprecedented pomp, style and emotion.

2. Angels – Robbie Williams

It must be the dream of any artist to have a song like 'Angels' as part of your repertoire. An irresistible melody which peaks in the chorus. The power of the song, which Robbie exploits live, is to personalise it by remembering someone you have loved and lost. Everyone can relate to this and the result is that the anthem is belted out by the throngs with supercharged emotion, making you feel good to be alive and part of something bigger.

3. Fix You – Coldplay

Another song about grief, written by Chris Martin to help his then wife Gwyneth Paltrow, cope with her father's death. The power is twofold. Firstly, the journey of losing a loved one is entirely relatable. Secondly, the composition of the song starting with the gentle mellow synth organ for the first two verses and then the crescendo of the swirling guitars and multi-part harmonies is stirring. Sung live by a choir of gig-goers only multiplies its effect, providing a catharsis of emotion and hope. An anthem to die for!

4. TOP 3 Special Moments

1. Coldplay - Charlie Brown - 2011

This was Dom's first ever gig. On the way in we were given wristbands that looked a bit like watches, and we weren't sure what they were. About a third of the way into Coldplay's set, they started to play the song *'Charlie Brown'*, which kicks in with a great riff. At the point of kick in, suddenly our wrist bands all lit up and started flashing coloured lights to the rhythm of the song. The sight of 20,000 flashing wristbands in the O2 arena is something I will never ever forget. It was incredible. This and similar gimmicks have been done to death since, but back in 2011 this was 'out there'. The surprise element and the spectacle make it probably the most memorable moment of any gig. Whenever I talk about this show with Dom or anyone one, I always refer to it as *'the gig when the lights came on'*.

2. Prince – Little Red Corvette - 1989

One of Kirsten & my 'special' songs is *'Little Red Corvette'* by Prince. This was out when we began our relationship in Australia in the early 80s. This was the peak of the MTV era, so the videos released with the songs were as well known as the songs themselves. The video to *'Little Red Corvette'* is very sexy, and there's a bit in the short instrumental part of the song when Prince does a short but fantastic choreographed breakdance.

When we saw him at the O2 the show was in the round. We were near the stage but at the back of the stage. The purpose of a show in the round is for the artist to perform equally to the crowd. On this occasion, although we could see, we were definitely at the back, with the majority of action over on the other side. However, during *'Little Red Corvette'*, right at the dance bit, Prince turned, ran across the stage to the back and down a walk way right in front of us and replicated the dance. Immediately after, he ran back and completed the song. It seemed like a personal gift for us. A lovely unforgettable moment.

3 = Jimmy Eat World - 2016

As mentioned in Chapter 65, I attended this gig with both my boys. On this evening, my health was good, my energy was good and I felt very alive. There was this moment half way through a song, when I was moshing away, totally caught up in the music. Suddenly I was aware of this moment, that I was doing what I was doing and able to do it. As I looked around, close by were both boys also moshing and singing their hearts out with light and joy. I bottled that moment of sheer beauty and togetherness and have returned to it on frequent occasions. I wonder if that's what heaven will be like? I hope so.

3 = 'The Alarm' Staycation Weekend 2022

It's interesting on review that all my chosen special moments involved family and friends, and experiencing certain moments with them. As detailed in Chapter 76, this was a time full of special moments, and what made them so special was just being with our friends, who are No. 1 Alarm fans, and seeing what a joy this experience was for them.

5. TOP 3 Powerful Moments

1. Queen - Love of my Life 2018

When Freddie was alive, there was always part of the show where he would sit side by side on a stool with Brian on acoustic guitar, and they would duet a couple of songs, one of which was always *'Love of My Life'*. The first tour following Freddie's death was with Paul Rodgers. For this particular song, Brian came to the front and performed next to an empty stool, with the audience singing most of the song. Very emotional. However, in the 2018 tour with Adam Lambert, it went a step further. Brian performed the song solo with the crowd's help and then suddenly in the last chorus, Freddie appeared on the screen and completed the song together with Brian before waving to the crowd and walking off slowly and fading into the background. The stunned crowd went ballistic, Brian was clearly moved and I was in tears.

It was brilliantly done and provided an incredible moment, because just for a few seconds, Freddie was back with us.

2. Fish - Forgotten Sons 1990

This was Fish's first tour as a solo artist. For an encore he performed a Marillion song called *'Forgotten Sons'*. It's a powerful song about the war between Britain and the IRA, and the recruitment of young civilian men to fight, marketed by the government as 'a career.' When this song was written, the IRA had exploded a bomb that killed four soldiers. At the time of this concert, some seven years later, the conflict was still ongoing as were the lives being lost. Fish gave probably the single most powerful performance of any song I've ever seen done – acted out in his own indomitable style, yet on this occasion, we were not only observing but somehow drawn into the song with all its raw emotions of grief and anger. At the end I felt exhausted, as if in some way I'd performed the song. Extraordinary!

"On the news a nation mourns you
Unknown Soldier, count the cost
For a second, you'll be famous
but labelled posthumous…"
   Forgotten Sons.

3. Athlete - Wires 2013

Athlete saved their best-known song until last at this gig. 'Wires' is a haunting song written by Vocalist Joel Pott's about his newborn baby, who was rushed to intensive care after a premature birth, and in 2006 it won them the Ivor Novello Award for "Best Contemporary Song". The track captures the fear and panic of living through an experience like that, but climaxes in the bridge with a burst of hope *'I see it in your eyes, I see it in your eyes You'll be alright'*.

After the song finished and while the band were taking their final bows, the crowd spontaneously took up the bridge again, and for probably at least five minutes everyone in the whole hall was singing, *'I see it in your eyes, I see it in your eyes You'll be alright'*.

The band drifted off stage one by one, leaving Joel Pott alone and just staring out at the crowd with tears in his eyes. After a short while he took off his guitar, and almost reverently laid it down on the stage, and then simply walked off with the crowd still singing. It was a wonderful moment and an unorthodox but amazing end to a gig.

6. TOP 3 'Take-off' Moments

What I mean by this is that occasionally a gig has a defining moment. This is really hard to describe. I'm not talking about a favourite or hit song being played but where suddenly the gig takes off and kind of lifts into another dimension. From experience it's not that common, but the result is always similar – a collective joy, energy and oneness.

1. Athlete – Shake those Windows

The band were celebrating the tenth anniversary of the album, *'Vehicles and Animals'*. This resulted in them playing more off this album than they normally would, including a song called *'Shake those Windows'*. Now, this in my opinion, is a fairly ordinary track. I doubt it would have got a look in if the focus was not on the album. Yet about half way through, something happened that seemed to move through the audience and lift us all to a new level of... how could I describe it? Intensity? Joy? Connection? Spirituality? The band responded and went into a great impromptu extended instrumental. At the end of the song, frontman, Joel Pott, admitted it was the best they had ever played that song.

2. Biffy Clyro – Bubbles

This gig was going well anyway but when *'Bubbles'* was played, although it didn't seem any different in quality or energy to previous songs, something tangible happened. Again, you could sense something which seemed to sweep across the arena, a bit like an unseen Mexican wave. Collectively the place erupted - it was quite extraordinary.

3. Coldplay – Sky Full of Stars

Coldplay it seems to me, have the knack of being ahead of everyone else as far as spectacle goes. I've already mentioned in the special moments section about the wristband lights at the O2 gig in 2011. That certainly was a great example of a 'take off' moment too. But another springs to mind during their Wembley stadium show on the 'Head full of Dreams' tour 2016. Don't get me wrong, this show was spectacular from the word go with a massive stage full of colour, but about halfway through the set, the band did '*A Sky Full OF Stars*'; a brilliant song starting with a piano intro, which then leaps into a rhythmic house-influenced electronic dance chorus that is impossible not to bounce, dance or at the very least tap your foot to. But played live, this song hit a new level and when the chorus kicked in, it was like the universe exploded: wrist lights came on, screens filled with colour, fireworks, swooping lights over the stadium, confetti - talk about sensory overload. It was like the whole stadium became airborne. Check out this same song on their 2022 tour – a step up again.

Coldplay

INSTRUCTIONS FOR QR CODES
Hold Camera on Phone over QR image and open link.
OR
Copy the link below into your browser tool bar on PC/phone: https://youtu.be/Fpn1imb9qZg

7. Top 3 Best Starts.

1. Queen – Procession
1. Michael Jackson – Wanna Be Startin' Somethin'

I can't decide this one:

Is it?...

The 77 Earl's Court Queen Gig - the lighting rig in the shape of a crown, slowly rising, with the theatrics

OR...

The 88 Wembley Jacko Gig - the appearance from nowhere. He's not there and then he suddenly is!

For a bit of fun, you get an opportunity to choose by witnessing what I experienced.

Queen

https://youtu.be/OMpv1ykBQSY

Michael Jackson

https://youtu.be/AGUS_5lqeq

2. Manic Street Preachers – 'Motor Cycle Emptiness'

The lights go out, the band walk on stage, pick up their instruments, James Dean Bradfield walks up to the microphone and says, *"Good Evening (Whatever City), we are the Manic Street Preachers from Wales and this is 'Motorcycle Emptiness'"*... a drum count of four beats and the song launches with Bradfield's piercing, haunting, powerful, multi-octave guitar riffs.

I have seen the Manics on several occasions now. They have tried different starts to their sets, but they always seem to return to this song. That's because with its pace, singalong chorus and wonderful guitar echoing licks - well it just works!

3. Fish – Chocolate Frogs

In the 2,000s Fish did a series of toned-down acoustic gigs in pubs and small venues. At a gig in Kingston upon Thames, he came on stage without the band, and started the set with a cappella rendition of *'Chocolate Frogs'* (one part of the epic *'Plagues of Ghosts'* song). It was bold, unexpected, courageous, different, powerful and impacting.

8. TOP 3 Live Vocal Performance

1. Freddie Mercury
Without question the best vocalist I have ever heard. Apparently, Freddie had a four octave vocal range, and was aptly described by rock journalist, Caroline Sullivan, as *"A force of nature with the velocity of a hurricane"*.

2. Alicia Keys
An unforgettable performance of *'New York State of Mind'* at the Brit awards in 2010. This was a duet with Jay Z but Alicia Keys' vocals left a scar in both Kirsten & my memories, in that if ever anyone talks about top vocalists, our minds default to this gig. Talk about 'feeling the earth move under your feet'.

3 Tom Chaplin
A pure piercing almost angelic voice, which when it unfolds with increasing power and hits climatic notes within songs, sends a shiver down the spine every time.

9. TOP 3 Drummers

1. Phil Collins/ Chester Thompson (Genesis)

The 'drum duets'/'battles' are sensational to have witnessed. Check out the footage below from 2007 where the battle starts on stools.

https://youtu.be/j8BU4KRJ2Eg

2.= Tal Bergman (Joe Bonamassa)
2.= Clem Burke (Blondie)

Two drummers, I can't separate. Both have their own unique style requiring incredible energy. Both mesmerising to watch and impossible to ignore.

3. Neil Peart (Rush)

Somewhere in the middle of this kit is a Neil Peart

With the size of this kit, how could he fail to get in the Top 3?

Not quite there but close behind...

Ben Parker (Calva Louise)
Let him loose on Peart's' kit and he'd be top 3 for sure!

10. TOP 3 Guitar Solos

1. Mark Knopfler – Sultans of Swing
The recorded album version is great but the arrangement of the live version has grown and developed over the years and is constantly changing. As opposed to the song just finishing with the solo, the vocal section morphs into a quieter instrumental part with different blends of piano & sax, out of which Knopfler's solo emerges, gradually building and climbing higher and higher, eventually reaching a high peak ending that fulfils every potential promise. See version played in 1992 below.

https://youtu.be/RFclpoxI_-M

2. Dave Gilmour – Comfortably Numb
What can you say? For the power and purity and the visual feast in which I experienced it.

3. Brian May – Bohemian Rhapsody
I don't think there's anything quite as legendary as this solo. Most people know it intimately and can probably sing it note for note or at least hum along to it.

I always count it a privilege to have heard Brian May play the solo live on many occasions. Both my boys have also seen it. I took my younger son to a special performance of *'We Will Rock You'*, the Queen stage musical. Brian was making a guest appearance at the end of the show. Sure enough he came up on a moving platform from under the stage amidst dry ice, playing the solo.

I am hopeful in fifty years' time, my sons will have earnt some bragging rights on this one, and will enjoy a full appreciation of having seen the real thing!

Note: Seems wrong that both Schenker's *'Rock Bottom'* and Bonamassa's *'Mountain Time'* don't feature in the top 3 - but now I've added this note, they kind of do!"

11. TOP 3 Support Bands

1. The Waterboys - Wembley Arena 1985
Opened for U2 at Wembley Arena and blew them away. I knew none of their stuff, but boy were they amazing! Fresh and full of energy and life.

2. Dry the River- The Roundhouse 2011
Supported the Manics at the Roundhouse. They were so unusual and different, and a band that stuck in the memory banks. I wasn't sure what I felt about them initially, but came to love them and was there at their headline show at the London Forum a couple of years later (c/f Chapter 61).

3. To Hell With Burgundy – UEA 1992
Don't know where they came from or where they went but this band supported *Barclay James Harvest* in Norwich in 1992. They used male and female harmonic vocals in a similar style to Paul Heaton and Jacqui Abbot, and were fantastic.

12. TOP 3 Disappointments

We're talking here of occasions when I've been really gutted, and in one case still am!

1. Queen – 1977

```
QUEEN INVITES YOU TO HELP
THEM MAKE A FILM OF THEIR
NEW SINGLE SOON TO BE
SHOWN ON TELEVISION.
 ENTRANCE IS FREE FOR YOU
AND YOUR FRIENDS BUT THE
HALL ONLY HOLDS 900 SO
SEATS WILL BE GIVEN TO THE
FIRST PEOPLE THERE. NO
ONE WILL BE ADMITTED ONCE         MEMBERSHIP NO 250083355
THE THEATRE IS FULL. FOOD
AND DRINK WILL BE ON SALE         DAVID PARKER
AND COPIES OF THE SINGLE          21 NORTH PARADE
ARE AVAILABLE FREE.               GRANTHAM
PLACE : NEW LONDON THEATRE        LINCS
        CENTRE,DRURY LANE,WC2
DATE : THURSDAY 6 OCT
TIME : 5.00 PM
HOPING TO SEE YOU THERE.

    AMANDA
```

After the Earl's Court gig, I became a member of the Queen Fan Club. A couple of months later, I got a postcard inviting me to be part of the filming of a video for their new single. The event was in London at the Drury Lane Theatre on a Thursday. I received the postcard the day before. The same problems confronted me as had initially with the Earl's Court concert – a school day and transport. Sadly, there was no way I could swing it at such short notice, and I had to let it go.

It turned out to be the new promotional video for *'We are the Champions'* and apparently after the filming the audience were treated to an impromptu intimate mini gig.

Whenever I come across the video for *'We are the Champions,'* I still feel a surge of disappointment.

Oh, Woe is me!

2. Gary Glitter - 1994

I had a friend staying with me from New Zealand who was a Gary Glitter fan and had never had an opportunity to see him live. He was over the moon when I managed to get tickets at Wembley Arena for the annual Christmas show. I hadn't seen Gary in such a large venue so it was bound to be a festive extravaganza. We arrived at Wembley in time for the support band – The Village People. I have to say, what a genius choice. What better way to get the crowd warmed up than some high-power singalong disco anthems from this camp sextet. *'In the Navy', 'Macho Man'* and of course *'YMCA',* left us nicely poised for the main act.

The lights went out, the intro music started the crowd went wild and then... nothing happened! We were aware of long introductions, but we waited and waited as the intro music continued and then... it stopped, the lights came on and a suited figure ambled onto the Wembley stage. He announced that Gary, in his warm up routine, had pulled a muscle, couldn't move and couldn't perform. My first thought was that this was a joke, but the awful realisation gradually dawned that it wasn't, and we gloomily headed back for a three hour trip home. We tried to put on a brave face and laugh it off, but the deep disappointment was unshakeable.

3. Michael Jackson – 2010

When this comeback tour was announced, I devised a plan to take my younger son Dom to this show for his first ever gig at the O2 London. I knew after experiencing the Wembley '88 show, it would be a memorable, never to be forgotten concert. On the day of the ticket sales, I joined a long online queue. I don't know how long I waited but it was over an hour. When it was my turn, there were no tickets left. But I kept trying through the day and around mid-afternoon, some suddenly registered as being available and I snapped them up. I didn't know what seats, what level or what section we would be in, nor did I care! We were going! Dom was ecstatic knowing MJ's hits through a DVD he had, so anticipation was already high. Then came the devastating news that Michael had died suddenly, and of course the whole tour was cancelled. Personal disappointment is hard but bearing your nine year old's too is not fun! As a small consolation we have the hologram ticket that was offered instead of a cash refund, as a memento.

13. TOP 3 Bizarre & Funny Moments

1. Foo Fighters & Rick Astley

Sometimes strange things happen and you wonder if you are really seeing what you are seeing. Such was an occasion in the middle of this FF gig. Dave Grohl proceeded to introduce a very special guest to the stage and lo and behold its Rick Astley, who then duets with the Foos in a storming, heavy rock version of 'Never Gonna give you Up'.

Rock n' roll history made right then and there!

2. Coldplay Wristband

I think the idea was that this wristband was handed in on exit after the show, but nobody did. After all, who would turn down free merch? About three or four nights after the gig, I had just gone to bed and turned the light out to sleep. Suddenly I was aware of a glow in the room. I looked around, and my wristband, which was still out on the dressing table, was mysteriously glowing and kind of slowly pulsating. It lasted about a minute then stopped. To my knowledge it never happened again although I put it away in a drawer after that. How or why, it happened I don't know – it was a little unsettling.

3. YMCA Leaving Wembley

Travelling home after the show will never be anyone's favourite part of gig-going. I often marvel at the larger venues and the organisation it takes to disperse a vast crowd; I have to say Wembley Stadium, who have one of the largest crowd numbers, also have one of the best organised exits. I guess they get plenty of practice. Anyway, following a Coldplay gig at the stadium, we were sardining it on a wide pathway slowly towards the tube station. At a higher level was another smaller path (not accessible to us) but there were three or four workmen/ contractors of some kind with luminous jackets, and they were watching the crowds streaming from the stadium. They had a radio on and just as we were passing them, YMCA came on the station they were listening to. Well, a few of the crowd started to sing and do the actions, and within a minute this had spread to thousands exiting Wembley. Everyone was singing YMCA and doing the moves. It was a funny and joyous moment and suddenly the journey home didn't seem so bad after all.

14. TOP 3 Artists I wish I'd seen

There are a few bands I have never seen and would love to have done – Oasis are one, Sparks are another, but the top three are as follows…

1. The Beatles
It's interesting that the biggest band in rock n' roll history, whilst prolific in touring until 1966, only ever played one gig between then and when they broke up in 1970. This was the well documented 1969 rooftop gig at the Apple Corps Building in London. The chances of me ever seeing them live never really existed. Of course, they make the Top 3 simply because they were and always will be the biggest band in the history of popular music.

2. Sunrise Avenue
I have, on several occasions, discovered new bands and on investigation found out that they are in fact not 'new' but have either been going for years or have already split up. I came across Sunrise Avenue, a band from Finland (led by vocalist/ guitarist Samu Haber) in 2022. True to form I find out after twenty years together, they are on a farewell tour and about to play their final ever gig in a large stadium in Germany. I don't know what it is about

this band but I never seem to tire of listening to their music; they have a heap of top tracks, some of which have become firm favourites [e.g. *Hollywood Hills/ Forever Yours/ Fairy tale gone Bad/ Not Again* etc], and having seen clips of their final tour on YouTube, I would have loved to have been there. I can only hope they have a 'Status Quo' perspective of a final/ farewell tour, in which case they'll be back on the road in a couple of years' time.

3. Joshua Kadison

Joshua Kadison is a US singer/songwriter/pianist best known for his massive hit in the early 90s *'Jessie'* (supposedly written about his relationship with *'Sex in the City'* star Sarah Jessica Parker). His debut album, *'Painted Desert Serenade'* was a commercial success which placed him very much in a 'Love Song Ballad' box. His follow up album, *'Delilah Blue'*, was totally different. It was a much more diverse record, combining a variety of styles from gospel to jazz to blues. The title track clocking in at just under ten minutes is in my top five songs of all time.

Kadison then went off grid, shunning the limelight and commercial success. Over the years, he released recordings on a low-key scale such as the brilliant *'The Venice Beach Sessions'*. The reason I wish I could see him live is not only the fact that I love his voice, but that I believe he is one of the best 'musical' storytellers, having the ability to make you laugh and cry in one song.[56] Unfortunately, outside a mega change of direction, there will be no chance of me ever seeing him play live.

---

[56] Check out *'the Bubble Man'*, *'Paris'* and of course *'Delilah Blue'*.

15. TOP 3 Photos with the Stars [57]

1. Frank Turner

2. Tom Chaplin

3. Mike Peters

---

[57] I should point out that these Top 3 are in fact the <u>only</u> 3

APPENDIX B

Index of Artists Seen Live

as a headline act, support slot or guest appearance.

A: AC/DC, Adam Lambert, The Alarm, Alicia Keys, All about Eve, Al Stewart, The Animals, Annie Lennox, Anvil, April Wine, Arcane Roots, Athlete, Axl Rose.

B: Barclay James Harvest, Beans on Toast, Biffy Clyro, Billy Squier, Blackfoot, Black Sabbath, Blazer Blazer, Blondie, Blue Oyster Cult, Bob Dylan, Bob Geldof, The Boomtown Rats, Bruce Springsteen, Bryan Adams.

C: Calva Louise, Chaz & Dave, Cheryl Cole, The Chicks, The Church, Cliff Richard, Coldplay, The Coronas, Curiosity Killed the Cat.

D: David Bowie, Def Leppard, Delirious? Dire Straits, Dizzie Rascal, Dry the River.

E: Eddie & the Hot Rods, The Editors, Elton John, Embrace, Emeli Sande, Enter Shikari, Extreme.

F: The Feelers, Fish, Florence and the Machine, Flogging Molly, Fogg, Foo Fighters, Foreigner, Frank Turner & the Sleeping Souls.

G: Gary Barlow, Gary Glitter, Genesis, George Michael, Gillan, Girl, Girlschool, The Glitter Band, Guns n' Roses.

H: Hanoi Rocks, Hawkwind, Heart, Hot House Flowers, The Howlers, Human League, Hunter & the Bear.

I: Ian Hunter, Iain Matthews, Idlewild, Imagine Dragons, INXS.

J: The Jam, James Dean Bradfield, Jason & the Scorchers, Jay-Z, The Jets, Jimmy Eat World, JLS, Joe Bonamassa, John Cooper Clarke, John Otway, Joan Jett, Jools Holland, Judas Priest.

K: Kasabian, Katrina & the Waves, Keane, Kim Wilde, The King Blues, Kodaline.

L: Lady Gaga, Led Zeppelin, Lianna De Havas, Liar, Lightning Seeds, Lily Allen, Linkin Park, Lisa Stansfield, Lulu.

M: Magnum, Manfred Mann's Earth Band, Manic Street Preachers, Margaret Urlich, Marillion, Mark Knopfler, Marseille, Mavis Staples, Meat Loaf, Metallica, Michael Jackson, Mick Ronson, Mike Peters, The Mission, Mud.

N: Nazareth, The New Barbarians, New Hearts, The Next Band, Nils Lofgren.

P. Pat Travers Band, Paul Rodgers, Paul Young, Peter Gabriel, Phil Collins, Pink Floyd, The Pirates, Pistol Kings, The Police, Prince.

Q: Queen.

R: Rainbow, Reef, REM, Rick Astley, Riot, Robbie Williams, Robert Plant, Rod Stewart, Roger Daltrey, Rush.

S: Sammy Hagar, Samson, Sandi Thom, Saxon, The Scorpions, Scouting for Girls, Seal, Dave Sharp, Sheryl Crow, The

Silencers, Simple Minds, Simple Plan, Slade, Slash, Southside Johnny & the Asbury Jukes, Squeeze, Starsailor, Status Quo, The Stranglers, The Supremes, The Sweet.

T: The Teardrop Explodes, 10cc, Thin Lizzy, Thunder, Todd Rundgren, To Hell with Burgundy, Tom Chaplin, Tom Jones, Tom Petty & The Heartbreakers, Tom Robinson, The Tom-Tom Club, Tony Iommi, The Troggs, T'Pau.

U: U2, UB40, UFO, Uriah Heap

V: Vega4, The Village People.

W: The Waterboys, Wet Wet Wet, Whitesnake, The Who, Wishbone Ash, Wonder Years.

Z: Zucchero, Zed.

There are omissions which tend to be mainly obscure support bands. I have not included Tribute Bands.

APPENDIX C
Acknowledgements

The high percentage of content in this book has been from my own recollections, diaries, gig journals and conversations with those that I have attended with. For this reason, there is bound to be the odd error, for example thinking an occurrence was in one gig when it was in another. If this is the case I sincerely apologise and blame it on age.

All images in the book, I have produced either by photos taken at the actual gig or of my ticket stub collection or from the original gig programme. There is the occasional image that is a screenshot from online gig footage. A couple of images used have been long term on my computer and I have no idea of the source.

Outside of that, the following people are accredited for the following images:

Chapter 7 Knebworth Crowd – Ove Stridh
Chapter 8 The Who – Vin Miles
Chapter 9 Freddie & the hands - David Edwards
Chapter 9 Venue photo - David Matkin
Chapter 19 Slade - Tommy Strauss

I acknowledge the following websites that have been helpful in supplying long forgotten details:

queenconcerts.com
queenlive.ca

ukrockfestivals.com
Setlist.fm

A special thanks to Ben Parker for the cover design and the artwork for the decade sections.

Also huge thanks to my chief editor, Susi Barber, and my wife who 'stepped up' beyond the call of duty.

I am also grateful to New Generation Publishers for pointing the way a second time.

My gig going companions over the years have been extensive and varied. I have only mentioned my wife, Kirsten and two sons, Ben and Dom by name. Some of my favourite moments are when I have been with them, and I have treasured memories some of which are recorded in these writings.

Regarding my other friends far and wide, I felt it would be way too confusing to name each person for each gig. However, I have attempted to compile a list of my gig buddies over the years. There are going to be omissions and if by any chance you read this and realise one of them is you, I sincerely apologise. A special dose of gratitude to those of you I am still in touch with and who have helped me stir up old memories.

And so, my love and thanks, (wherever you are) go out to:

Tim & Helen Angell, Richard Anscombe, Mike Argyle, John & Susi Barber, David Baxter, Paul Baxter, Phil Gumby - Biggs, Andy Coulson, Matt & Tracey Gray, Andrew Harrod, Chris Hart, Cliff Healey, Sue Hilli, Frances Howe, Adrian Howse, Suzi Kowal, Audrey Lau, Liz Lawrence, Leong KF, Nigel Lilly, Alan Marshall,

Michael & Mavis Parker, NG Kim Poh, Tim Norris-Jones, Jo Pawsey, Simon Pitkethley, Andy Ramage, John Reynolds, Brian Smith, Jimmy Tang, Derek Tay, Bill Taylor, Stuart Wakerley, Brendan 'Codger' Wall, Simon 'Algy' Wingfield.

Milton Keynes UK
Ingram Content Group UK Ltd.
UKHW032035011124
450529UK00003B/82

9 781835 631997